A Funny Thing
Happened on the Way to the
Broadcast Booth

A Funny Thing

Happened on the Way to the

Broadcast Booth

by
Steve Albert

AUFREY PRESS
New York

Copyright © 2025 Steve Albert

All rights reserved. No part of this book may be reproduced, distributed or transmitted in any form or by any means, including photocopying, recording, or other electronic or mechanical methods, without the prior written permission of the publisher, except in the case of brief quotations embodied in critical reviews and certain other noncommercial uses permitted by copyright law. The book reflects the author's present recollections of experiences and conversations over time. Some events have been compressed and some dialogue has been recreated. For permission requests, write to the publisher, addressed "Attention: Permissions Coordinator," at the address below:

>Aufrey Press
>380 Lexington Avenue, 31st Floor
>New York, NY 10168
>www.aufreypress.com

Publisher's Cataloging-in-Publication Data:
Names: Albert, Steve, author
Title: A funny thing happened on the way to the broadcast booth/Steve Albert; foreword by Bob Costas.
Description: New York: Aufrey Press, [2025] |
Identifiers: Library of Congress Control Number: 2024925637 (print) | ISBN 979-8-9921094-9-8 (Hardcover) | ISBN 979-8-9921094-8-1 (Paperback)
Subjects: LCSH: Albert, Steve | Sportscasters—United States—Biography | Sports—Professional Sports | Sports—History | American Wit and Humor—Humorous Stories. BISAC: SPORTS & RECREATION / Essays | HUMOR / Sports & Recreation
Classification: LCC GV707.A43 2025 | DDC 796.0973

First Edition | April 2025

Printed in the United States of America

Cover Design: N.W. Wong
Cover Photo: © Michael Chow – USA TODAY NETWORK
Editors: Rich Mintzer, Sara Putnam and Linda LiDestri
Photos Used with Permission by BSE Global; Bob Costas, Cliff Gelb, Golden State Warriors, Good Karma Brands LLC, *THE GRUDGE MATCH* ©1991 20th Television (All rights reserved), International Boxing Hall of Fame, George Kalinsky, MTV, NBCUniversal Media, LLC, Phoenix Suns, Professional Sports Publications, Showtime Networks, Inc., Abby Sims, WWOR-TV, Inc., N. W. Wong, Steve Albert, and Albert Family Collection

This book is dedicated to my brothers, who inspired me to become a sportscaster, and to my parents who supported me in my journey.

I also dedicate this book to all my broadcasting colleagues and friends—and to the memories of those I've lost through the years. We had a lot of laughs.

Finally, to my first broadcast booth. A little room in Brooklyn, where all the "fun and games" began.

Table of Contents

Foreword by Bob Costas i
Introduction 1
Help! I'm Locked in My Bathroom! 5
It Wasn't Funny at the Time 9
My Oddest Broadcast Booths 19
Survival of the Fittest 25
Duck! 33
It's Checkout Time 37
Flying the Not-So-Friendly Skies 41
O Say, Can You See 49
Did This Really Happen? 51
Dream Job 67
Name Dropping 77
Living Through History 89
Starting Kent State Hockey 99
What Do I Do? 115
Breaking the Ice 123
Tall Stories 131
A Learning Experience 149
Monty, Monty, Monty! 153
Punchlines 155
The Bite Fight and Other Chunks of Boxing History 167

Boxing's Highest Honor	181
I'm Ready for My Close-Up	191
Tastes Great. Less Filling!	203
Just When You Thought I Had Done It All	209
My First Broadcast Booth	217
What's in a Name?	233
Mom, Dad, and Brooklyn	237
Marv, Al, and Me	253
It's All Relative	267
Epilogue: After the Broadcast Booth	273
Acknowledgments	275
About the Author	277

Foreword by Bob Costas

Sometime in the early '90s, Marv Albert was a guest on *Later*, the wee-hours interview show I hosted on NBC. At one point, the conversation turned to the many branches of the Albert family sportscasting tree. There was Marv of course, fabled voice of the Knicks and the NBA on NBC. Brother Al Albert, the versatile hoops, hockey, and boxing announcer. And Marv's son, Kenny, then just beginning his career in New York and on network TV.

"Yes," said Marv, "we are very proud of Kenny."

"And what," I inquired, "about your youngest brother, Steve?"

"Yes," Marv intoned, "We are concerned about Steve, who for the past year has traveled the country as a puppeteer."

A Funny Thing Happened on the Way to the Broadcast Booth

Turns out, that was not true. But, dear reader, you are about to learn that, all things considered, had it been so, it would not have been the most unusual or amusing chapter in Steve's career, much of which is rendered in entertaining fashion on the pages that follow.

Here's something Steve and I have in common: Many of our best stories come from similar episodes in minor leagues or leagues long since defunct. Broadcasting minor league hockey into a telephone because anything more elaborate isn't in the budget? Check. Harrowing drives through snowstorms in rattling jalopies or broken-down team buses? Check. Coach's or team owner's wife as your broadcast partner? Check. At the mic when arena riots broke out? Check: Me in the old Eastern Hockey League, inspiration for the Paul Newman movie *Slap Shot*, Steve at various prizefights where the violence was not confined to the ring. Lifetime membership in the Voices of Defunct Leagues Club? Check. In that category, though, Steve has me at least four to one: He has the World Hockey Association, World Team Tennis, and the World Basketball League. And both of us were part of the late, great American Basketball Association. In fact, Steve and his brother Al (sorry, Marv) both called the last game ever in the ABA, game six of the 1976 Finals, Steve for the Nets of Dr. J, Al for the Nuggets and David "Skywalker" Thompson.

If ever a league embodied both the ridiculous and the sublime, it was the ABA, which provided both highlights and hijinks on a regular basis. For a broadcaster, it offered a free ticket to the circus, a treasure trove of anecdotes and memories, and experiences both beautiful and bizarre. And since those chapters came while we were young and impressionable, they resonate all the more decades later.

One more: Steve writes about an errant pass by LeBron James ricocheting off his head. Well, during the '98 Eastern Conference finals on NBC, Dennis Rodman dove for a loose ball at midcourt and wound up knocking me ass over tea kettle and into the first row of seats at Market Square Arena in Indianapolis. So . . . check.

Foreword by Bob Costas

To tell you the truth, until I read *A Funny Thing Happened on the Way to the Broadcast Booth,* I never realized how much Steve and I had in common. We have to get together more often. If only Marv would stop monopolizing my time . . . so annoying.

Anyway, turns out Steve's a darn good writer. This is a rollicking read, telling tales of a Brooklyn household with three budding sportscasters under one roof (two playing ping-pong while the third called the action), the Hamster Olympics (let Steve explain), Brooklyn street games, and a Boomer's bonanza of references to *The Honeymooners, The Ed Sullivan Show, The Rifleman, Winky Dink and You* (don't ask), and Claude Rains, *The Invisible Man.* Because, why not?

Steve's story is brimming with humor, insight, and good nature. I think you will enjoy it as much as I did.

— Bob Costas

A Funny Thing Happened on the Way to the Broadcast Booth

Introduction

Introduction

Funny things happened to me during my decades in sportscasting. After years of being crammed into broadcast booths and sitting courtside for basketball games or ringside for boxing, I wanted to share with you the weird, wacky, and downright bizarre things that happened on my way to and in the broadcast booth.

I recall some great, and some not so great, moments in sports, from trying to find words to describe Mike Tyson chomping off part of Evander Holyfield's ear during the infamous Bite Fight to keeping an interview going with Mickey Mantle while the Yankee legend did everything in his power to distract me.

I recount getting stuck in a bathroom shortly before airtime and trying not to laugh when my broadcast partner accidentally set his chair on fire. I also introduce to you the many colorful stars and personalities I met along the way. And, I share my memories of growing up in 1950s Brooklyn as one of three future sportscasters in one household.

Despite not knowing exactly where it all was going, my brothers and I began to hone our craft at home. We all seemed to have the same dream, to announce the sports we loved to watch.

I turned pro in college. Then, for forty-five years, calling games was my life—and also my brothers'. I think it all worked out.

My oldest brother, Marv Albert, became one of the most recognizable sports voices in history and arguably the greatest basketball announcer of all time. My older brother, Al Albert, had a long and distinguished career as a play-by-play man for the National Basketball Association and the National Hockey League and spent eighteen years as a nationally known boxing commentator.

Me, the baby of the family? I was supposed to be a cartoonist. At least, that's what my brothers thought. When I entered the same field as Marv and Al, they considered it an upset. Truth be told, I knew all along what I wanted to be when I grew up. There was never any doubt in my mind.

Looking back, I loved every minute of it. Well, almost every minute.

I did play-by-play for just about every sport you can imagine. By my count, I called games for thirteen teams in eleven leagues. We're talking *Guinness World Records* stuff here. Early in my career, I announced in six leagues that do not even exist anymore, including something called the World Football League, which folded in its second year, and the Major Indoor Soccer League, where so many goals were scored, I was suffering from whiplash.

I plied my trade with four teams in the NBA, primarily with the New Jersey Nets, and won an Emmy in my last stop, with the Phoenix Suns. I guess I finally got it right. I announced for more than twenty years for *Showtime Championship Boxing*, doing blow-by-blow for some of the biggest fights in boxing history. I even made it into the International Boxing Hall of Fame, the World Boxing Hall of Fame, and the New York State Boxing Hall of Fame.

Introduction

I was privileged to have a multifaceted career, appearing in numerous movies, dramas, and sitcoms, along with many television and radio commercials. I was the host and play-by-play announcer for the long-running MTV *Rock N' Jock* series, working with dozens of major celebrities and sports heroes. As one of my childhood idols, baseball announcer Mel Allen, would say, "How about that!"

I hope you enjoy these stories about my early life and my work as a sportscaster. You don't need to know the names of all the participants or the rules of the game to find them entertaining. Many of the stories are funny, but you'll also find a dose of drama, some history, a walk down memory lane, and even a life lesson or two.

A Funny Thing Happened on the Way to the Broadcast Booth

Help! I'm Locked in My Bathroom!

I had a lot of jobs in broadcasting, but working the morning shift in the early 1980s on WABC radio in New York was probably the most gratifying. Morning drive time was the premier slot on radio, since commuters stuck in traffic were always listening. The audience was appreciative, and I sensed that program director Mark Mason always had our backs. I think management understood how hard we worked and that we genuinely wanted to deliver a high-quality show.

The host of the show was a successful stand-up comedian named Alan Colmes, one of the most talented people I've ever worked with. My role was to announce the latest sports scores and news briefs every fifteen minutes. Since no games took place during these hours, I reported primarily on the games played the previous night. There was rarely breaking news, unless some team fired a coach at 6:00 a.m., which never happened on my watch. Time permitting, Alan and I would chat about various subjects, often collapsing in fits of laughter. In addition, my contract called for me to do play-by-play for the New York Jets.

I loved the working environment and my broadcast colleagues at the radio station. The hours, though? That was another story. I had to wake up in the middle of the night, five days a week.

I usually went to sleep about 9:00 p.m., with my alarm set for 3:30 a.m. I never really adjusted to the crazy hours. Let's just say I learned to deal with it. One night, I was asleep in my apartment when I heard what I thought was my alarm go off. It felt like I hadn't been asleep very long, and I felt cheated.

I dragged myself out of bed and slumped to the bathroom. I brushed my teeth, showered, shaved, and put on my clothes. When I got back to the bedroom, I glanced at the clock and couldn't believe what I saw. It said 11:00 p.m. I rubbed my eyes, shook my head, and looked at the clock again. Still eleven o'clock.

Then I heard a noise from outside. It sounded like the noise my alarm clock made when it went off. Only it was a car alarm from down on the street. Apparently, whenever I heard an alarm, any alarm, I was so conditioned to the routine that I jumped out of bed and went about my business without thinking, as if I was in some sort of trance. I had slept a grand total of two hours. No wonder I was still so tired.

So, now what? I'm showered, shaved, dressed, and ready to go to work, but it's 11:00 p.m. I peeled off my clothes, put my pajamas back on, and went back to bed. I wasn't going to miss those precious four-and-a-half hours of sleep. When the alarm went off at 3:30 a.m., I made sure it was definitely my alarm clock before I got up. Even then, I spent a few seconds listening to make sure no car alarms were going off.

* * *

Help! I'm Locked in My Bathroom!

One very cold winter morning, I got up as usual at 3:30 a.m. and headed into the bathroom to take a shower. When I was ready to get dressed, I went to open the bathroom door. The doorknob was loose and jiggly. As I turned it, the knob spun around and around, and the door wouldn't open.

I tried to remove the pins from the door hinges, but they were impossible to budge. It was at this point that I officially realized I was locked in my bathroom.

I began to go into panic mode. I needed to get out of that bathroom. I then had to drive from my apartment building in Fort Lee, New Jersey, over the George Washington Bridge, onto the West Side Highway, and through the streets of midtown Manhattan to get to the radio station in time. This was years before cell phones, so I couldn't call anyone. I probably wouldn't have had my phone in the bathroom anyway.

I looked around and spotted a big aerosol can of hairspray. I grabbed it and started pounding it on the wooden door, which I soon discovered was very thick and heavy. Slowly but surely, I managed to batter a hole in the middle of the door, which, after I smashed away for several more minutes, was big enough for me to climb through. Or so I thought. Halfway through, I got stuck. All I had on was a towel around my waist.

So, there I was, part way through the jagged hole, trying to figure out if I should attempt to wriggle forward or back. It seemed less perilous to slide back, so that's what I did. Very carefully.

I was right back where I started. Now, even more furiously, I hacked away at the door with the can of hairspray, trying to make the hole larger. Can you imagine the racket? BANG! CRASH! BOOM! at 4:00 a.m. They probably heard me in Hackensack.

I was ready for take two. I began again to crawl cautiously through the hole. Once I got my rear end to the other side of the door, it was just a matter of carefully sliding my body down to the floor. The spiked edges of the hole looked like shark's teeth.

A Funny Thing Happened on the Way to the Broadcast Booth

Finally, I made it out. As I got to my feet, I discovered wood chips in body parts I hadn't even known existed.

I was so focused on leaving that I forgot to call the station. I threw on some clothes and set a land speed record from Fort Lee to the ABC building in Manhattan. I was late but, surprisingly, missed only the 5:45 sports report.

Alan Colmes looked at me and said, "What happened?" He could see that I was disheveled and disoriented, still picking wood chips out of my hair. I proceeded to give him the "headline" version, to which he replied, "Okay, forget the sports this morning. I want you to sit down here in the studio with me and tell this entire story on the air, and don't leave out one detail. Not one."

Within seconds of my finishing the story, the station's phones lit up with calls from listeners who couldn't wait to tell their own tales of getting locked in their bathrooms, basements, and garages. I couldn't believe how many people had similar experiences. They came out of the woodwork, so to speak. The phones continued to light up as the mass confession went on.

It was a happy ending to a nerve-racking ordeal. To this day, I never go into my bathroom without my cell phone—or a big can of hairspray.

It Wasn't Funny at the Time

Holding down several sportscasting jobs at the same time made my life hectic, but it never caused any major problems until one near-calamitous event prior to a hockey telecast.

For most of my career, I always seemed to be working at least two jobs, sometimes three. My brothers, Marv and Al, did the same, and now Marv's son, Kenny Albert, continues the tradition. Kenny is the longtime radio voice of the New York Rangers, the lead NHL play-by-play announcer for TNT, and calls National Football League and Major League Baseball games for Fox Sports, among other sportscasting gigs. I don't know when he sleeps. In one stretch, he called a Rangers game on a Friday night, a Knicks game on Saturday afternoon, another Rangers game Saturday night, and on Sunday afternoon, a Giants football game—four games in three sports in less than three days. In college, I once announced three separate sporting events—hockey, wrestling, and basketball—on the same day. Perhaps it's a family affliction.

When the Islanders won the first of four straight Stanley Cups in the 1979-80 season, I was announcing their home games, while the venerable Tim Ryan did the away games. Hockey writer Stan Fischler and former Islander captain Ed Westfall partnered with us. I also had a "desk" job as a television news sports anchor.

The men of the family. Back row from left to right are Al, Marv and me. Front row is my nephew Kenny and my father Max. This was well before Kenny had to get to a game.

I spent a number of years, as did my brothers, in this other genre of sportscasting. Instead of calling the action on a three-hour sporting event, I was allotted three or four minutes to summarize the entire day in sports.

I worked at different times at WCBS-TV (Channel 2), WNBC-TV (Channel 4), and WOR-TV (now WWOR-TV) (Channel 9), all New York area stations. Through the years at these various stations, I could be found on the six, ten, and eleven o'clock news, making happy talk with the news anchors and meteorologists.

It Wasn't Funny at the Time

Initially, WCBS-TV hired me to report sports on weekends. I had succeeded the talented Len Berman, who went to WNBC-TV where he had a long and successful run. Those were big shoes to fill. My on-air colleagues included news anchorman John Tesh and weatherman Irv Gikofsky. John became a Grammy-nominated musician who composed the iconic NBA on NBC basketball theme, "Roundball Rock," and co-hosted *Entertainment Tonight*. Irv, better known as "Mr. G," has been a popular fixture on the New York television scene for decades. I had an outstanding behind-the-scenes production team, with Doug Grabiner, Cliff Gelb and Carmine Cincotta. I also got to rub shoulders with the one-and-only Warner Wolf, who did weekday sports.

On Saturday nights, after the news broadcast, I co-hosted a pre-taped interview program called *Sportspeople* with ex-hockey great Phil Esposito, and on Sunday nights following the news, I hosted a live feature show called *Sports Update*, which wrapped up the week in sports. My plate was full.

While anchoring weekend sports on WCBS-TV, I co-hosted *Sportspeople* with former hockey star Phil Esposito (left). Here, we interviewed New York Yankees announcer Phil Rizzuto (middle) at his home.

While the on-air exposure was advantageous, I felt more comfortable on-site at a sporting event than in some stuffy newsroom. I was more of an in-the-trenches guy. I hungered to be where the action was. Maybe it was in the blood.

There were periods in my life when I did play-by-play and sports on the news at the same time. When I was announcing for the Islanders on SportsChannel, I was also employed by WCBS-TV on their weekday 6 o'clock news broadcast. I knew when I got involved with both the Islanders and WCBS-TV, I was playing with dynamite, from a logistical standpoint. However, neither the team nor the TV station objected, so I thought, "Why not?" I felt I could handle the two assignments. Well, juggle them.

My brothers and I when we were all sports anchors at WNBC-TV, Channel 4 in New York. We teamed with producers Dave Katz and Len Zaslowsky.

The newscast was from 6:00 to 6:30 p.m. My segment ran from just after 6:20 to about 6:25. Islanders home game broadcasts got underway at 7:30 p.m.

It Wasn't Funny at the Time

The CBS Broadcast Center was in Manhattan on West 57th Street between 10th and 11th Avenues. The Nassau Coliseum was in Uniondale, Long Island, some thirty-four miles away. I usually had just about an hour to travel, in rush hour traffic, from door to door, or, more accurately, from anchor seat to announcer's chair in the broadcast booth.

It sounds insane, particularly if you know New York traffic. Yet somehow, I made it work. I must add, it wasn't without some help, and for that I thank Steve Paulus, then a young production assistant at WCBS-TV.

Steve was a die-hard New York Rangers fan. Despite that, he was gracious enough to volunteer his services to the announcer for the archrival Islanders. Every time I had to call a game out on the Island, Steve would leave the newsroom just before I started my sportscast, go get my car out of the nearby parking garage, and bring it around to the front entrance of the broadcast center. He knew my predicament and what I had to go through to get to the Nassau Coliseum in time to call the games. He told me later he had seen that it was turning me into a wreck and was afraid I was headed for heart failure. Out front, Steve kept the motor running so I could make a quick getaway.

Every second counted. We had the process down to a science, and it saved me a lot of time. Nobody but the two of us knew why Steve disappeared every evening from 6:15 until 6:30. His work for the newscast was finished by then, so he didn't get into hot water. I don't know what I would have done without him. Thanks to Steve and some crazy driving, I never missed the start of a game, but I did have my share of close calls.

I knew I was living on the edge, and one night it almost caught up with me. The game was a showdown between the Islanders and the Montreal Canadiens, which meant a sellout crowd and traffic, traffic, traffic.

As I drove toward the coliseum, I realized that I was cutting it close. It was now dark, making matters even dicier.

Inching along in the traffic on the Grand Central Parkway (which turns into the Northern State Parkway), I could just make out the faint silhouette of the arena in the distance. In my best Marv Albert impersonation, I exclaimed, "Yesss!" That glee immediately turned to gloom as my car abruptly came to a standstill. It was bumper to bumper, cars backed up for miles.

The time was now 7:15 p.m. The broadcast would start in fifteen minutes, with or without me.

This was before everyone had a cell phone—I couldn't just call the producer from my car. I banged my head on the steering wheel in frustration. I struggled to peel off my overcoat, then my suit jacket, to change into my SportsChannel garb. Anybody looking into my car must have thought I was being attacked by a swarm of insects.

"I'm doomed," I thought. "There's no way I can make it." Then, magically, out of nowhere, a dirt shoulder appeared. How far it went was of no consequence to me. I was desperate.

I swerved the steering wheel, drove over the median line, and bolted down the narrow lane. I was Steve McQueen in the chase scene in the movie *Bullitt*. I heard horns honking. Staring straight ahead, I disregarded the many profanities coming from the other drivers.

Flooring the gas pedal, I sped along at eighty or ninety miles an hour, kicking up a trail of dust and holding onto the wheel for dear life. Thank goodness the makeshift road ran all the way to the coliseum parking lot. I don't know how I did it, but I parked and ran like a wild man to the press entrance of the Nassau Coliseum.

Once inside, I galloped, overstuffed briefcase in hand, all the way around the end zone toward the other side of the arena, where the broadcast booth was located. It was 7:29 p.m. I could see the TV lights turned on and my color analyst, Stan Fischler, preparing to open the broadcast alone.

I dashed up the stairs and literally dove into the booth. Stan, a big smile of relief on his face, handed me the microphone. I hastily put in my earplug and heard the producer count down "five, four, three, two, one, go."

"Hi everybody, this is Steve Albert along with the Hockey Maven, Stan Fischler, and welcome to New York Islanders hockey!"

To all you budding play-by-play announcers out there, I don't recommend that you do what I did. If you're ever in such a situation . . . rent a helicopter.

So, whatever happened to Steve Paulus?

He went on to be one of the architects and founders of NY1, the twenty-four-hour news channel that became an indispensable source of news and information. He also helped launch the Spanish language news channel NY1 Noticias as well as fifteen other all-news channels across the Time Warner Cable system, all modeled after NY1 and serving millions of viewers from California to Texas to upstate New York. He would oversee all of them as senior vice president of news and local programming for Time Warner Cable. Last I heard, he's still a die-hard Rangers fan.

* * *

Less than two years after announcing my first college hockey game, I found myself on the threshold of calling my first professional hockey game. I was a senior at Kent State University in Northeast Ohio, a stone's throw from Cleveland.

Joe Tait, the radio voice of the Cleveland Cavaliers, was one of the all-time great NBA play-by-play announcers. Back in the '70s, Joe used to moonlight, announcing selected Springfield Kings games. The Kings were in the American Hockey League, the level just below the National Hockey League. WMAS radio in Springfield, Massachusetts, used regional announcers for Kings road games rather than hiring a full-time voice, I presume as a cost-saving measure.

A Funny Thing Happened on the Way to the Broadcast Booth

Occasionally, Joe had a scheduling conflict. That's where I came in. Joe knew of my work calling Kent State hockey and one day asked me if I could fill in for him.

What Joe didn't tell me was that these hockey games were not broadcast with a microphone, a headset, or a radio engineer by your side. The play-by-play was done solo, on a landline telephone. I was so thrilled at the prospect of announcing a game in the AHL, I would have done it with two paper cups and a string while standing on my head.

I was to be paid $250. Don't tell anybody, but I would have paid them $250 to do it, if I'd had it.

Joe was kind enough to throw me another game in Cleveland, and they must have liked my work in Springfield because they asked me if I would be available to call a third game in Hershey, Pennsylvania, with the Kings squaring off against the Hershey Bears.

Hershey was 310 miles from Kent, or about a four-hour and forty-five-minute drive. I didn't have a car or a clue about how I would get to the game, but I immediately accepted the assignment.

When I mentioned my dilemma to Mike Fornes, my Kent State hockey broadcast partner, he said, "Why don't you use my car?"

I asked, "Are you serious? You'd let me borrow your car?"

He replied, "Yes, on one condition. You take me with you to Hershey to be your statistician."

"You've got yourself a deal."

Like me, Mike was a hockey worshipper. He had been a stick boy for the Dayton Gems of the International Hockey League. (Stick boys are hockey's counterparts to baseball's bat boys.) We were birds of a feather who would jump through fire to work a hockey broadcast. The Hershey game was on a Saturday night, and I lucked out in that it did not conflict with Kent State's hockey schedule. Despite the fact that a blizzard was forecast for the Midwest, Mike and I set out early Saturday morning with plenty of time to get to Hershey.

Mike drove a 1962 Chevy Nova that his dad had bought used in 1971. As I got behind the wheel, Mike mentioned that the car had a few mechanical problems. One was a broken speedometer. Not too serious, we would just have no way of knowing how fast we were going on the turnpike. However, Mike said, it did have a great cassette deck, which allowed him to turn up the music loud enough that he didn't hear the terrible noises the car made.

Years later, Mike confessed that he was lucky to be alive after driving that rattletrap in Ohio's winter weather. The car broke down so often on the interstate that he had to learn how to replace tires, belts, and hoses, and add radiator fluid to keep it going.

Despite this less-than-perfect scenario, I was determined to get to Hershey for the broadcast.

The storm turned out to be much worse than anticipated. As the white-knuckle trek unfolded, the snow got heavier and more blinding. At least the windshield wipers worked.

The broken speedometer was a moot point. We moved along at a snail's pace. The roads were icy and extremely hazardous, and neither Father Time nor Mother Nature was on our side.

As if the driving conditions weren't horrendous enough, about halfway through the trip, Mike started to feel ill and crawled from the passenger seat to the back seat. He didn't lose his lunch, but he later told me he felt like he would, due to the fumes from the bad muffler. Only after we returned to Ohio did Mike learn that he had scarlet fever, and he ended up spending five days in the Kent State Health Center.

No, it wasn't pretty. I drove with one eye on the road and the other on the Hershey Bears roster, which I was desperately trying to memorize.

A fortune cookie once told me, "It takes courage to move forward when the outcome is uncertain." Whether it was courage, *cajones*, or craziness, we made it.

The blowing snow made it difficult to see, but we knew we had arrived in Hershey. All the streetlamps were shaped like Hershey's Kisses. At that point, I could've kissed the hood of the Nova.

A Funny Thing Happened on the Way to the Broadcast Booth

We got to the Hershey Arena parking lot, trudged through the snow, and made it into the building moments before the opening face-off.

Once inside, I sprinted for the finish line. Sucking wind, I hurtled into the broadcast booth and frantically dialed the number the radio station had given me.

Within seconds, I was on the air, calling my first road game as a pro. "Hi everybody, this is Steve Albert, and welcome to Springfield Kings hockey!"

Despite the torturous trip, I wouldn't have traded that experience for anything. Well, maybe just the part where Mike got sick. I'm happy to report that Mike survived scarlet fever and the drive to Hershey, and eventually made it to the NHL as a play-by-play announcer.

I don't think either one of us will ever forget that day. We weren't laughing at the time, but we can chuckle about it now. It was grueling, but our experience taught us the truth of an old broadcasting axiom: There's nothing quite like genuine, hands-on, practical experience. Sure, you can learn a lot in a classroom, but nothing beats the real thing.

I'm not suggesting that you drive through a blizzard in a decrepit vehicle, but it's by working behind a microphone, or even on a telephone, that you finally get the feel of calling a game.

On top of that, knowing you can meet difficult challenges—weather related, mechanical, or anything else—can give you the confidence and poise to tackle almost anything.

It never occurred to me for a second that I was not going to make it through that storm in time for the broadcast. That day, I learned unequivocally how I was wired, and I would apply that fortitude and passion throughout my career. These qualities, combined with the preparation habits I developed later in life, such as making in-depth team charts and extensive game notes, served me well. If only I had those attributes in high school, I might have been a Rhodes Scholar. I'll say this: After that trip to Hershey, I was a Road Scholar!

My Oddest Broadcast Booths

You think the National Hockey League was the first to come up with the idea of playing outdoors? I was scheduled to announce a Kent State game at Oberlin College, a private liberal arts school in Oberlin, Ohio. The KSU Hockey Club, including their trusty play-by-play man, arrived via a caravan of station wagons. We were like a new rock band that had not yet graduated to a tour bus. Much to my surprise, Oberlin played its home games on an outdoor rink—in the Midwest, in the middle of winter.

    A canopy provided some coverage, but the sides and end zones were completely exposed to the elements. I noticed that there was no broadcast booth. I was informed that I would be calling the game while standing in a tiny cubicle at ice level. It's a good thing I was broadcasting solo. A color commentator would have had to sit on my shoulders. A phone line and headset mic were set up in the make-do booth for the broadcast from the studios of WKSU, the campus radio station. On top of that, I was located right next to the side-by-side penalty boxes for the two teams. It was a recipe for disaster.

Bundled up in my parka, scarf, and gloves, I started my play-by-play. At first, things went well—different from what I was used to, but fine. As the game went on though, there was a dramatic shift in the weather. The temperature plummeted and it began to snow. As the arctic blast ramped up, my play-by-play became shiver-by-shiver and I froze from head to toe. It made today's NHL Winter Classic look like a day at the beach.

It wasn't as unpleasant for the players, who skated speedily around the rink in their bulky gear. The cold wind pierced through me as I stood, teeth chattering, in my cubicle at the edge of the ice. The snow accelerated and within minutes erupted into a full-scale blizzard. The players kept on playing, and I kept on announcing. Snow accumulated on the ice to the point that they could have stopped playing hockey and started a snowball fight. It was snowing sideways, rendering the canopy useless.

As Ron Popeil, the famous TV marketing personality, used to say, "But wait, there's more!" In the midst of this blinding squall, a fight broke out on the ice. I remember saying into the mic that the two players had purposely dropped their gloves so they could hug each other for warmth.

In any event, the referee doled out the penalties, and the penalized players from Kent State and Oberlin skated to their respective penalty boxes, right next to each other. One of the boxes was within arm's length of my broadcast position. Nothing separated the sin bins—the two players were so close they might as well have been sitting in the same box. Within seconds after the ensuing face-off, I could hear the two guys jawing away. The exchange got louder, and it wasn't exactly G-rated. As I covered the mic to keep the colorful language from the airwaves, the verbal dispute escalated into fisticuffs, spilling over into my pint-sized broadcast booth.

Dodging haymakers and fending off out-of-control hockey sticks, I continued trying to announce the game. Where's a goalie mask when you need one.

To make a long story longer, the fight was eventually broken up, the game mercifully came to an end (we won, 2-1), the freezing cold and snow raged on, and to my knowledge, Kent State never again played an outdoor hockey game. The NHL could keep that tradition all to themselves.

* * *

There's an old saying that those who can't do, teach. In my case, those who can't do, announce.

In my freshman year, my college roommate, Greg Benedetti, and I tried out for the KSU baseball team. We both did not make the squad. My consolation prize was that I got to announce for them.

On the outskirts of the Kent State University campus sat Allerton Field, home of the KSU baseball team. It was also home to a dilapidated yellow school bus which was parked along the first base line. That was our broadcast booth.

The wheels were gone, so at least we had no fear of being hijacked during the game, and the seats had been removed. My radio partner, Wayne Lynch, and I kept our audio equipment, scorecards, and notes on a wood plank installed under the windows.

We sat just to the left of the big steering wheel. One game, there was a little more action than we anticipated, and it wasn't taking place on the field. It was happening in the bus—I mean, broadcast booth.

While we were on the air, we noticed a hornet's nest hanging near the rearview mirror. We continued to announce the game, praying that the hornets would remain inside. When a line drive foul ball slammed the side of the bus, the hornets suddenly awoke and started to buzz around in anger. We tore out of that heap faster than any player could run the first base line.

A decade later, I was in the big leagues announcing for the New York Mets, where the only buses involved took us from hotels to ballparks to airports. I can honestly report I never saw another hornet's nest in a bus or, for that matter, in a broadcast booth.

Both Wayne and Greg also became broadcasters. Greg, a Beaver Falls, Pennsylvania native, went on to work as a sportscaster in Pittsburgh and Beaver, Pennsylvania. Wayne switched from sportscasting to newscasting. Those pesky hornets in the school bus had nothing to do with it. He became a news anchor in Baltimore, Maryland, then a news director in Richmond, Virginia. Along the way, he wrote a book about the 1967 NBA champion Philadelphia 76ers, bringing his love of sports full circle.

* * *

The Mets added 1969 World Series champion Art Shamsky to their broadcasting team, just in time for the 1981 Major League Baseball strike, which meant no MLB games were played during the dispute.

To fill the programming void in New York and to provide viewers with a baseball fix, SportsChannel sent Art and me to Tokyo, Japan to call a couple of games between the Yomiuri Giants and the rival Hanshin Tigers.

We were warmly welcomed by everyone—players, journalists, fans, and even Giants' assistant manager and former superstar player Sadaharu Oh, the world's homerun king. Then, we were escorted to our broadcast booth, which consisted of two seats and a table in the stands behind home plate.

I never asked why they placed us down near the field instead of the regular broadcast booth higher up. Maybe the local broadcasters had dibs on the booth. Art and I didn't complain, especially during our pregame preparation when, much to my surprise, an exceptionally long line of young fans was waiting to say hello and to get our autographs. It was endearing and we stopped what we were doing to greet them. Each fan approached us one by one and bowed, as was their custom. We signed autographs like the "superstar" announcers that we were (or at least felt like we were).

Every once in a while, an odd broadcast booth had its perks. In fact, I remember thinking, maybe the baseball strike will never end.

A Funny Thing Happened on the Way to the Broadcast Booth

Survival of the Fittest

When I worked Mets games with Bob Murphy and Ralph Kiner in the late 1970s and early 1980s, we didn't have the separate radio and television broadcast teams that most baseball fans now know. We took turns, two doing the TV side while the other worked the radio booth. It wasn't unusual between innings to see Bob, Ralph, and me scrambling around the press box from one booth to the other so we would be ready to call the first pitch after the commercial break. Who knew I would be announcing and exercising at the same time? It's amazing that there weren't a few collisions. I can see the headline now: "Albert Trampled by Kiner in Broadcast Booth Crash."

Working with Ralph Kiner was a trip. Ralph had been a prolific home run hitter for the Pittsburgh Pirates who was such a huge star in his day that he once dated actress Elizabeth Taylor.

A Funny Thing Happened on the Way to the Broadcast Booth

Ralph played only ten years in the major leagues. His career was cut short by injuries, but he nevertheless won seven straight National League home run titles and slugged his way into the Baseball Hall of Fame. Almost singlehandedly, he restored the faith of Steel City baseball fans following World War II.

After his playing days were over, Ralph made the transition to the broadcast booth. Before long, he became famous for his on-air slips of the tongue, which were known as Kinerisms. These slips might occur while he was doing play-by-play or hosting his popular postgame show, *Kiner's Korner*. For example, as Mets catcher Gary Carter strode to the plate, Ralph often referred to him as Gary Cooper. Then there was "On Father's Day, we again wish you all happy birthday." How about "The Hall of Fame ceremonies are on the thirty-first and thirty-second of July." There was the time he said, "Hello, everybody, welcome to *Kiner's Korner*," then forgot his name.

During one game when Mets reliever Neil Allen was warming up in the bullpen, Ralph was due to toss it to me to call the action. Ralph said, "And now for the play-by-play, here's Steve Allen." For you youngsters, Steve Allen was the original host of *The Tonight Show*. He was a talented guy. He was funny, played piano, and wrote music and books. I don't think play-by-play was in his repertoire, although I wouldn't have put it past him.

* * *

The Mets struggled mightily during my brief but memorable time with the team. They were so bad, I once had two Mets tickets in my car, and someone broke in and left four more. One day, during another long and arduous season for the fans and the announcers, the Mets were hosting the St. Louis Cardinals at Shea Stadium. It was solely a radio game, no TV. Therefore, it was Ralph Kiner, Bob Murphy, and me smooshed into the radio booth, sitting shoulder to shoulder to shoulder. In those days, the out-of-town scores came to us by ticker tape, and we would periodically report them on the air. The ticker-tape machine was right behind us in the booth. It made a ticking sound as the narrow paper strip containing the scores and game information fed down into a circular wastepaper basket. As the tape accumulated, it would eventually become a large ball of paper.

Arthur Friedman, our statistician, would empty the basket of the used ticker tape, then put the basket back next to the machine. Art the Dart, as he came to be known, had worked as a stat man with my brother Marv at Madison Square Garden. I was lucky to work alongside him with the Mets.

During games, Ralph would often light up a big cigar and proceed to puff away. When it was his turn to do the play-by-play for this Mets-Cards game, Ralph lit up one of his stogies. As he announced, he flicked the cigar ashes into the wastepaper basket where the ticker tape was piling up. He slid the basket closer to his chair several times to make it easier to flick the ashes into it. Eventually, the basket ended up under his seat. While he was calling a fly ball to left field, the ticker tape in the wastepaper basket caught fire, erupting into flames that engulfed his chair—and his rear end. Ralph leaped into the air mid call and screamed, so startled that he abruptly stopped his play-by-play. Bob jumped in, "As Ralph was saying . . . that fly ball to left field is caught by Dane Iorg."

I bit my tongue hard to keep from laughing but couldn't hold it for long. I howled. To our right, the Cardinals announcers, Jack Buck and Mike Shannon, were roaring hysterically. It was one of the zaniest things I had ever witnessed in a broadcast booth, and it gave new meaning to the term "being in the hot seat." Something like that could only happen to Ralph Kiner, who truly was one of a kind. Whether he meant to or not, Ralph took the edge off those tedious seasons with the Mets. I'm not sure what we would have done without him.

* * *

A Funny Thing Happened on the Way to the Broadcast Booth

The closest I ever came to a facial fracture during a broadcast was a night I was announcing a Suns-Cavaliers game in Cleveland. Our broadcast position was courtside, adjacent to the Suns bench. The only thing in front of us was the basketball court.

The Cavs had a player by the name of LeBron James. You may have heard of him? LeBron was standing on the court just a few feet from me. He fired a scorching pass to what he thought was one of his teammates standing near the sideline right in front of our table. The only problem? There was no teammate standing near the sideline right in front of our table.

As a result of this misconception, the basketball zoomed toward my left eye. Did I mention that I was wearing eyeglasses? At the instant the ball made contact with my glasses, I was reading a promo printed on an index card—BAM! The bullet pass to the Invisible Man twisted and mangled my spectacles, rearranging them on my face from horizontal to vertical. My headset followed, repositioned from horizontal to vertical on my head and face. That is what you call an unusual two-pointer. Had he knocked my drink off the table as well, it would have been a three-pointer.

Frankly speaking, it was an errant pass, unless of course LeBron mistook me for a teammate. If so, he needed glasses more than I did.

The heat-seeking missile stunned the daylights out of me. It was traveling with such velocity that even my broadcast partner, former player Eddie Johnson, couldn't deflect it.

Everyone—players, coaches, fans—was looking in my direction. The fans around me were buzzing. However, despite my disorientation, I finished reading the promo on the air. After gathering myself during the next commercial break, I came back on and said, "Folks, I just got back from concussion protocol, and I've been cleared to continue."

I'm still waiting for flowers from LeBron. I'd settle for a card.

* * *

Sam Adkins was not exactly a household name in the world of boxing. A journeyman fighter, Adkins was a burly six-foot-three heavyweight who once fought on a Showtime undercard but didn't make the television broadcast. Only the few die-hard early bird fans in the stands saw the fight at the Thomas & Mack Center in Las Vegas. Sam was going against a six-foot-five behemoth named King Ipitan.

I wasn't paying much attention to this preliminary bout as I sat ringside readying for the televised event. My preparation habits were quite meticulous. In addition to thorough researching, studying video, and meeting with the fighters and trainers, I would write out reams of notes, or ad-libs, as I jokingly called them, on legal pads with a felt-tip pen. At each fight, I would carefully place these gems on the broadcast table amidst all the wires, cables, and TV monitors.

Ad-libs in place, I would then precisely line up my trio of beverages—coffee, water, soda—on the far edge of the table closest to the ring apron. This ritual persisted throughout my career.

While arranging these items on the table, I saw, out of the corner of my eye, King Ipitan land a titanic haymaker on Sam Adkins, knocking him clear through the ropes directly above me. In what looked like super slow motion, Sam slithered down the ring apron onto the broadcast table. He took down the TV monitors, wires, cables, and all three of my scrupulously placed beverages. The flying liquid drenched my notes, and the ink began to dissolve, turning words into watercolor blobs, rendering them virtually unreadable. I had spent weeks preparing the notes. My tools for the broadcast were decimated, just like that.

As Sam continued to slide, destroying everything in his path like Godzilla in Tokyo, he landed briefly on my lap before descending further to the cold concrete floor. There he sprawled in a daze, looking directly at me. I felt so bad for him. Yet, what did Sam do? He smiled. Then, he shook it off, struggled to his feet and got back into the ring. He may have lost by disqualification in the final fight of a 2-7 career but, to me, Sam Adkins was a winner because he had the heart of a champion.

A few minutes later, one of the Showtime production assistants rushed out to ringside with a portable hair blower, and we were able to salvage most of my notes.

He never made the live broadcast, but the image of Sam Adkins is indelibly etched in my mind and on my lap.

* * *

While I was the radio voice of the World Hockey Association's Cleveland Crusaders, I also did the play-by-play of selected road games on television. WUAB-TV hired a woman named Sue Needham to serve as my color commentator. Sue was the wife of the Crusaders coach, Bill Needham.

My biggest worry at the time was Sue's ability to be objective on the air. However, she was surprisingly honest about the Crusaders.

As the season unfolded, though, I developed another concern. While Sue maintained her neutrality, every time the Crusaders scored, in her exuberance, she would sharply elbow me in the ribs. If this had taken place down on the ice, she would certainly have been assessed two-minute penalties for elbowing.

I considered wearing goaltender pads under my shirt to absorb the blows. Instead, I braced for the jabs whenever Cleveland lit the red lamp and merely grimaced after each call of "He shoots, he scores!" Sue was a terrific analyst and her energy was contagious. Nonetheless, I may have been the only announcer in hockey history who did not mind if his team was shut out.

* * *

When Bobby Hull, also known as the Golden Jet, brought his booming slap shot from the NHL's Chicago Black Hawks to the WHA's Winnipeg Jets in 1972 by signing the first million-dollar contract in hockey history, it opened the door for other stars who jumped leagues.

After Hull, the legendary Gordie Howe, Gordie's sons Mark and Marty, and other standouts like Derek Sanderson, Bernie Parent, and Gerry Cheevers followed suit.

Cheevers, nicknamed Cheesy, joined the Cleveland Crusaders after a stellar career as a goaltender for the Boston Bruins. Cheesy was very popular in Beantown and soon became a fan favorite in Cleveland. He stood out clearly on the ice, wearing a white goalie mask painted with black stitch marks, depicting what he might have looked like had he not worn face protection.

Cheesy was an engaging personality who often stumped me in sports trivia contests during our travels on the road.

After a Crusaders victory in which Cheevers played brilliantly, I raced down to the ice to do a postgame TV interview with the ace goaltender.

Everything was going along smoothly when suddenly I felt a little queasy and my hand started to shake. In the middle of our conversation, Cheevers asked, "Steve, are you okay?" Apparently, the rubber cover of the microphone cord that was lying on the watery ice had torn open, exposing the copper wires, which were sending shockwaves through the mic into my body. That was, literally, the most "electrifying" interview of my career.

A Funny Thing Happened on the Way to the Broadcast Booth

Duck!

Of all the sports I announced, none held a candle to boxing when it came to fan uprisings, usually triggered by controversy. That was never truer than on one particular Seat Cushion Night at a bull ring in Mexico.

When the marketing people conceived the idea of seat cushions as giveaways, I think they were meant for sitting, not soaring.

When the opponent of the crowd favorite was handed an unpopular decision, the aficionados were not pleased and expressed their feelings by hurling the cushions like Frisbees toward the ring.

The seemingly innocuous giveaways zinged down in an avalanche. Fighters and trainers covered their heads and scrambled for safety. It was some sight. Seat cushions were everywhere. Many of the cushions whizzed into the ring after deflecting off my noggin at ringside. If only they had combined Seat Cushion Night with Helmet Night.

A Funny Thing Happened on the Way to the Broadcast Booth

* * *

One oppressively hot and humid afternoon at an outdoor venue in Mexico, the sun was baking the Showtime broadcasters and the capacity crowd. Many of the patrons had begun imbibing early, and by the time a particularly contentious decision by the ringside judges occurred, a large number of them were both inebriated and irate. It was not a good combination. As soon as the judges' scorecards were announced, all hell broke loose. They flung bottles and glasses toward the ring. Unfortunately, we were out in the open, pressed up against the broadcast table with very little room to move our legs. While we realized we were not the objects of their derision, we also understood the term "collateral damage."

As the deluge of objects intensified, our steadfast producer David Dinkins Jr. implored us through our headsets to get under the table. We were in such a tight squeeze, we couldn't budge, so I did what any clearheaded blow-by-blow announcer would do—I pulled off the fastest wrap-up in boxing broadcasting history. After my abrupt "So long, everybody," we were rescued by security people, who ushered my Showtime colleagues and me to safety.

* * *

A ring riot in Stuttgart, Germany, topped them all. It was a showdown between hometown hero Axel Schulz and South Africa's Francois Botha for the vacant International Boxing Federation heavyweight crown. I'll always remember this day for a variety of reasons.

The drive to the arena from our hotel in the former East Germany took us all the way along the remains of the Berlin Wall. To see it for the first time in person was sobering, and we asked our driver to slow down so we could take it all in. Much of the concrete was still intact, but people were now able to walk freely around the wall and through its openings. The multicolored graffiti on portions of the wall was gripping to see. There were so many messages of peace and freedom. It was hard to believe that it hadn't been that long ago that the wall still stood, separating communist East Berlin from democratic West Berlin. It was a profound experience.

When we arrived at the arena, I found it difficult to focus back on boxing. It seemed so trivial after what we had just seen. Following our preshow meal and last-minute preparation, I headed out to our ringside position, ready to call the action. I was settling into my seat at the broadcast table and arranging my notes when the lights suddenly dimmed. In his inimitable style, ring announcer Michael Buffer proceeded to introduce legendary singer Meat Loaf, who climbed into the ring to perform his hit song "Paradise by the Dashboard Light," in a duet with a female vocalist.

Starting in opposite corners of the ring, they came together to serenade the crowd, while just a few feet away at ringside I got ready for the broadcast. What a day! First, an unscheduled tour of the Berlin Wall, then a small slice of "meatloaf."

If that wasn't enough, it was also Listerine Bottle Night. Complimentary bottles of Listerine mouthwash were handed out to the eleven thousand fans in attendance that evening. Were they trying to tell these people something? The bottles, thank goodness, were plastic, not glass.

After a couple of preliminary bouts, Ferdie Pacheco, aka the Fight Doctor, and I finally got around to announcing the main event. The unbeaten Francois Botha of South Africa won a questionable split decision over Axel Schulz, and the fans were incensed. I could feel the eruption coming. Fans flung beer, wine, champagne, and yes, those plastic Listerine bottles, at the ring. They threw some coins in for good measure.

Schultz was hoping to become the first German fighter to win a heavyweight championship belt since Max Schmeling had beaten Jack Sharkey some sixty-five years earlier, but he lost. Once again, I heard those "comforting" words in my headset from producer David

Dinkins Jr.—"Get under the table"—as projectiles zoomed around me. My back was to the crowd, and my skull was a perfect target.

Thank goodness our stage manager, Joel Farbstein, was standing close by my side, diverting bottles and coins. A female spectator just to my right was lying on the floor, blood oozing from her head. She could have used the Fight Doctor's medical attention, but he had already been dispatched to the dressing rooms for post-fight interviews. I was told, make that ordered, to wrap it up and "get out of Dodge." I shattered the speed record for the fastest sign-off in boxing history, breaking my old mark in Mexico. Like our friend Meat Loaf, I was a "Bat Out of Hell."

It's Checkout Time

When I was a play-by-play announcer for the Mets, there was nothing quite like an extended road trip. It could be a four-city jaunt over fifteen days. Packing? What a pain in the you-know-what. The travel itinerary was the size of *War and Peace*.

On one of those unending odysseys, I was thrilled to see the light at the end of the tunnel. After a series in Cincinnati, we had thankfully arrived at our final destination. With my last ounce of energy, I dragged myself to my room and collapsed onto the bed. When I woke up the next morning, I had no idea where I was and had to ask myself, "Where am I?"

"We just came from Cincinnati," I thought. "That much I remember. But where are we now?" I had heard about this syndrome from players and other announcers, but I had never experienced it. It was scary. I thought the answer would come to me if I just waited another moment or two. Nothing. Not a hint.

As embarrassing as the prospect was, there seemed to be only one way out of this quandary. I had to work up the nerve to call the hotel operator to ask a question I had never asked before: "What city am I in?"

I slowly picked up the phone and dialed 0 with my shaky index finger.

A woman's voice on the other end blurted, "Bonjour!"

After a few seconds of dead silence, I yelled out, "Oh my god, I'm in France!"

The operator said, "Calm down sir, you're not in France, you're in Montreal."

Just then, it all crystalized. I remembered that it was a three-game set against the Expos. I was so relieved, I treated myself to a celebratory room service.

What did I order? French toast, of course.

* * *

The days of metal hotel keys were finished, gone the way of the dodo bird. The future, in the form of a credit card-shaped piece of plastic, stared me in the face.

It was easy enough to use. Even a dope like me could slide it into the slot. But the key (sorry) to getting into the room was making sure you had the *right* key. Duh.

One night, I announced a New Orleans Hornets (now the Pelicans) basketball game in Milwaukee, the first of back-to-back games. The next night's game was in Chicago. We arrived in the Windy City late at night and schlepped our weary bones into the hotel lobby to pick up our room keys.

Players, coaches, announcers, trainers, and luggage were packed like sardines in the elevator. We all inhaled to make ourselves skinnier as the elevator car ascended. Of course, it stopped on every floor. By the time we got to the last stop, way up top, all that remained were a bunch of play-by-play guys and color

It's Checkout Time

commentators. The elevator door slid open and we dispersed, hauling our bags down the hallway toward our rooms.

I grabbed the key from my pocket, stuck it in the slot, and waited for the little green light to flash, signifying that I had mastered the art of unlocking a door. But the little light refused to go green, instead stubbornly glowing a radiant red. I tried again. And again. And again. After about ten attempts, I gave up. My compadres, witnessing this exercise in futility, were of no help. In fact, my frustration was a source of hilarity for them.

I used the hotel phone near the elevator to call the front desk and requested another key. They said it was so late that there was only one bellman working, and he was occupied with another guest. So, I got back into the elevator with all my bags, in case they put me in a room on another floor, and went to the front desk to get a new key. It was now closing in on two o'clock in the morning, and I had to be up in a matter of hours to start preparing for the game broadcast that evening.

It turned out that the lone bellman had just arrived back at the front desk, and he was nice enough to help transport my belongings back to the room.

When we got to the door, I reached into my pocket for what I thought was the new key and put it into the slot. Again, the light remained red. The bellman said, "Try it again." Still red.

He said, "Let me look at that key." He examined the key, then said, "Sir, do you realize where you are?

"Of course, I know where I am. I'm in Chicago."

"And where were you last night?"

"Milwaukee."

"Look at the key you put into the door." It read, "The Pfister Hotel in Milwaukee."

The moral of the story: Always throw out your room key from the previous hotel before traveling to the next city.

* * *

A Funny Thing Happened on the Way to the Broadcast Booth

One of my television partners was a fellow most people don't usually associate with broadcasting: Phil Jackson. People forget that before he won those eleven NBA championships as head coach of the Chicago Bulls and the Los Angeles Lakers, he was a TV analyst for the New Jersey Nets.

I first came into contact with Phil well before my broadcasting career got underway, when he played for the Knicks and I was a Knicks ball boy. Who knew when I was tossing towels to Phil and handing him water that I would wind up announcing with him? Not only did I call games with him, but on one road trip with the Nets, I wound up sharing a room with him.

It happened in San Diego, where the Clippers played prior to making their home in Los Angeles. When the team arrived there, they learned that the hotel was short on rooms. Nets trainer and traveling secretary Fritz Massman asked the players, staff, and broadcasters to double up.

Ordinarily, each person, from players to coaches to announcers, had his own room.

When Phil and I got to the room, I said, "Don't expect me to throw you any towels or serve you water. Those days are over, pal."

I always felt, had Phil decided to stay in television, he would have gone on to be a topnotch network color commentator for as long as he wanted. Coaching, however, was in his blood. As history proved, he made the right choice.

Flying the Not-So-Friendly Skies

One season during the World Hockey Association playoffs, the Cleveland Crusaders were pitted against the Houston Aeros, who had the league's biggest name, Gordie Howe, on its roster. Mr. Hockey, as he was known, played an amazing twenty-six seasons in the NHL and six in the WHA. He was one of the greatest players who ever lived, scoring 801 goals, an NHL record that stood until it was broken by Wayne Gretzky.

Normally, the teams flew on commercial flights. To cut costs, the league had decided to charter just one plane for the two teams. Both teams would fly on the same aircraft back and forth between Cleveland and Houston, which was most unorthodox.

A Funny Thing Happened on the Way to the Broadcast Booth

After the first two games of the series in Houston, we were all on the plane heading back to Cleveland. The Aeros were seated in the front half of the plane, the Crusaders in the back half. The only thing separating the two teams was a curtain. Cleveland got the best of this deal because the only lavatory on the plane was in the back, behind the last row of seats. The back of the plane was Crusader country. Every time a Houston player had to use the bathroom, he had to walk past all the Crusaders.

Hockey players, particularly back in those days, favored beer as their beverage of choice after games. You can probably deduce that the lavatory was a popular destination.

After we were in the air for a short while, the curtain slowly slid open. One of the Aeros looked around and saw nothing but a sea of smiling Crusaders. He started the long walk to the lav.

With every step he took, a Cleveland player sitting in an aisle seat stuck his foot out into his path. The Aeros player stumbled his way to the back of the plane, not making a sound or making eye contact. Can you imagine an all-out bench clearing, or in this case seat-clearing, brawl erupting between the teams? The Aeros tripped over Crusaders' feet all the way to the bathroom and back. Instead of a flight attendant, they needed a referee. Unfortunately, there was no penalty box. The hijinks went on for the entire flight. Every time an Aeros player opened the curtain to head to the bathroom, and it was often, he was in for the trip of his life. Make that "trips" of his life.

The Crusaders were relentless. Not one Aeros player was exempt from the foot follies. Then, just before we were to begin our descent into Cleveland, the curtain slowly slid open again. (Feel free to insert your own dramatic music here.) There he was, Mr. Hockey, God himself, Gordie Howe, and he didn't look pleased. Gordie started to make his way down the aisle, and guess what? That's right, hockey fans, not one Crusader extended his foot. Like Moses parting the Red Sea, Gordie walked a clear, unobstructed path to the bathroom.

Flying the Not-So-Friendly Skies

After Gordie emerged from the loo, he again walked unimpeded toward the midsection of the plane. When he reached the curtain, he turned around and looked back at the Crusader players, who were all staring at him, mouths agape. With a big smile and an even bigger wink, Gordie turned around and walked off into the sunset like John Wayne, the personification of sports nobility.

* * *

I could never sleep on airplanes. In my profession, that's not a good thing. When you travel as much as I did, getting enough Zs is crucial. Falling asleep in the middle of a broadcast could be embarrassing. Fortunately, that never happened. I can't vouch for the viewers.

Prior to a flight from New York to London for a Showtime boxing telecast, somebody suggested Ambien to solve my problem. Ambien, for the uninitiated, is a prescription sleeping pill. I had never taken one before and had no idea of its potency. Nobody told me I was supposed to take it when I first sat down on the plane. When to take it seemed a moot point as I felt kind of drowsy as we taxied to the runway. I thought I might actually doze off without help.

A couple of hours went by, and there I sat, eyes wide open, staring straight into the back of the seat in front of me. There were still about four hours before we arrived in London. I looked around and everybody was asleep. The stranger next to me rested his head comfortably on my shoulder. Comfortable for him anyway. Adding insult to injury, he was snoring. Despite my displeasure, I didn't have the heart to wake him up.

I thought to myself, "This is as good a time as any to try this stuff out." I fished around in my briefcase and pulled out the little plastic bottle of Ambien. I popped a tiny white pill into my mouth, took a swig of water, and waited. Fifteen minutes went by, a half hour, an hour. Nothing. Nada. No effect. I figured that the experiment had failed.

As the plane taxied to the terminal at Heathrow Airport, I woke up in a fog. Fitting for London, I suppose. I recall wondering how a pill that small could be so powerful. As we came to a complete stop, everyone stood up to collect their belongings. I literally couldn't move. I thought I was still sleeping.

Thankfully, Showtime had a couple of brawny ex-New York City policemen on our production crew, each of whom grabbed one of my arms and carried me off the plane, the tips of my toes scraping along the floor enroute to baggage claim. How I managed to get through customs is still a mystery to me. I looked and sounded like comedian Foster Brooks, who made a living on television and in nightclubs portraying a drunk, calling himself the Loveable Lush.

We somehow made it to our waiting car and were whisked to the hotel. New York's Finest assisted me to my room and gently placed me on my bed, and the next thing I knew, it was morning.

All I can say is, thank goodness this was before phone cameras and social media.

* * *

Flying has never been my favorite activity. While I always cherished what I was doing for a living, I never quite warmed up to the flying part. In other words, I loved being *on* the air, not *in* it.

Unfortunately, flying came with the territory. It was a major aspect of the job, and there was no way around it. Professional basketball teams used to fly commercially. Today, teams are shuttled around in private charter planes. There's no question that flying charter is much more comfortable and makes life easier. Not being a great flier, though, whether it was a commercial flight or a private charter, I was still fighting the demons.

Once during the 1975–76 American Basketball Association season, the Nets decided to do something out of the ordinary. They booked a charter flight for a game against the Pacers in Indianapolis, Indiana. You might say the Nets were ahead of their time. However,

Flying the Not-So-Friendly Skies

after what transpired, you might also say we couldn't wait to get back on commercial airplanes.

The flight started out calmly enough. It had been a smooth takeoff, and we were at cruising altitude. The plane, which was quite luxurious, was frequently used by rock bands. Its interior was different from anything I had ever seen. Each person had his own oversized first-class seat that swiveled, which was great for the players with their long legs. Legroom was always a major problem on commercial flights. There were tables throughout the cabin, and at the back of the plane was a built-in couch. We were flying in style and happy to be aboard. Yes, even me. I had more than enough room to spread out my team charts to prepare for that night's game. All was well, or so we thought.

After about a half hour, something caught our attention. We were all looking out the windows, and we noticed smoke coming from one of the wings. It wasn't ordinary, run-of-the-mill smoke. It was blue. I had never seen anything like it before while flying. We were all slightly concerned at that point. I remember the look on Bill Melchionni's face. Bill was a steady, dependable guard for the Nets, but I think it's safe to say that this may have rattled him a tad, and I couldn't blame him for being uneasy.

We continued to watch the colorful smoke streaming from the wing. All I knew was that it didn't seem right. It turned out that I was on to something.

An orange blaze joined the blue smoke coming out of the wing. Concern among the players was growing. I looked over at John "Super John" Williamson, who was sitting near me. Supe, as he was also known, was built like a tank and was one of the most fearless players in the ABA. He had pulled his wool hat down over his eyes. That visual did not do wonders for my confidence.

Finally, the pilot, who I recall was speaking with a German accent, came on the PA system and said, "Uh fellas, we're going to make an unscheduled landing in Harrisburg, Pennsylvania." Unscheduled landing? That was a nice way of saying "Start praying." I thought to myself, "Why did I leave Cleveland?" I had left my job announcing hockey there to join the Nets. Like a mantra, I kept repeating, "Why did I leave Cleveland? Why did I leave Cleveland?"

The plane's altitude was dropping, and I couldn't look out the window anymore. Everyone in the plane was totally silent. My guess is that we were all thinking the same thing: "Please land this thing. Just put this bucket of bolts on the ground." We felt the wheels come down. At least *they* were working.

I shut my eyes. The plane got lower and lower. Then . . . touch down.

It was a safe landing. That was the good news. As we taxied in, there was a collective sigh of relief. We looked at each other and smiled. The bad news? We still had to get to Indy for a game that night, which meant getting back on a plane, which at that point didn't sound too appealing.

There was no aircraft available that was large enough for the entire team, so they booked two planes, a pair of small Beechcraft 99s. I had never heard of, much less seen, a Beechcraft 99. They're not big. Basketball players tend to be big.

Almost everyone, including me, was reluctant to get on board, but what choice did we have? I remember standing on the tarmac near where the two small planes sat side by side and hearing Super John address head coach Kevin Loughery.

Supe said, "Coach, I'm not getting back on a plane."

Kevin said, "Yes you are, Supe."

After some cajoling, Super John lived up to his nickname and climbed aboard. I knew how he felt. I didn't want to get back on a plane either, especially one of these things.

Half the team went on one plane, half on the other. I happened to be on the plane with the great Julius Erving. The six-foot-seven Dr. J was sitting in the first row. There was so little legroom that his legs were literally protruding into the cockpit, nearly intertwined with the pilots' legs.

I didn't know whether to laugh or cry. Fortunately, in the end, it was the former.

We made it to Indianapolis. As it turned out, the Nets were so grateful to be alive after that ordeal that they beat the Pacers handily, and my broadcast partner, Bob Goldsholl, and I were so giddy we had one of our best broadcasts. That said, I remember thinking that next time I could be just as motivated by less drama. A lot less.

A Funny Thing Happened on the Way to the Broadcast Booth

O Say, Can You See

As a result of announcing so many sporting events through the years, "The Star-Spangled Banner" is ingrained in my head. Still, there's no way I could stand in front of a crowd of 15,000 and sing it by myself. No matter how many times I've heard our national anthem, I always marvel at the men and women who perform it flawlessly. It is not an easy song to sing.

I'm surprised it doesn't happen more often, but every once in a while, there's an anthem malfunction. One in particular stands out for me.

It happened in Oakland, California, before a Golden State Warriors game that I broadcast. Native son Huey Lewis, lead singer for the group Huey Lewis and the News, was on hand to perform the pregame ritual.

He got off to a nice enough start. Everything was going along smoothly when all of a sudden, about halfway through, he jumbled the words. Huey stopped and acknowledged the miscue. His hometown fans were more than forgiving. They gave Huey the benefit of the doubt and encouraged him to get back on the horse and gallop to the finish line.

Huey started again from the top. About halfway through, it happened again. He forgot the words. This time though, Huey was smart. He laughed it off and simply yelled out in his famous husky voice, "Okay, everybody, sing it with me!" The sellout crowd of fifteen thousand-plus cheered loudly, and in full throat, they finished "The Star-Spangled Banner" with Huey Lewis. That may have broken the record for most backup singers in sports history. Huey turned an awkward situation into a feel-good moment thanks to a spur-of-the-moment decision. But that's one time Huey Lewis could really have used the News.

* * *

Then there was the first, and presumably last, time I would see and hear "The Star-Spangled Banner" performed by, are you ready for this? A dummy. That's right, a dummy.

Do you remember an act known as Willie Tyler and Lester? Willie Tyler was a talented ventriloquist, and Lester was his inanimate sidekick. They were hired to sing the anthem before a New Jersey Nets contest I was announcing at the Meadowlands Arena. Even more hilarious, they set up two standing microphones.

I'm not sure which was more intriguing to watch, the two of them performing the anthem or the fan reaction to the two of them performing the anthem. There was a constant murmur from the crowd throughout the performance.

At least Willie and Lester didn't forget the words. And if they did, who would you blame?

Did This Really Happen?

How many people can say they announced the final game in the history of a league? How about two announcers from the same family being able to say that? It happened in my first season as the television play-by-play man for the New York Nets.

The American Basketball Association premiered in 1967. It was a maverick league that got in the face of the more established NBA. They had the audacity to use red, white, and blue basketballs and introduced the three-point shot. These were progressive marketing ideas that seemed blasphemous to old-school hoops fans. On top of that, their run-and-gun style and disdain for defense made the NBA cringe.

Going into the ABA playoffs in 1976, the Denver Nuggets were the best team during the regular season, with an impressive sixty wins. The New York Nets finished second with fifty-five. Denver had beaten the Kentucky Colonels in a hard-fought seven-game series to get to the finals. The Nets outlasted the San Antonio Spurs in game seven to make it to the championship round.

New York was led by the incomparable Julius Erving, better known as Dr. J, one of the greatest and most electrifying players of all time. The Nets also boasted the physically punishing Super John Williamson. They had the perfect head coach in the savvy South Bronx, New York, product Kevin Loughery, a former standout for the old Baltimore Bullets. It was said at the time that if you wanted a coach for one game, one very important game, Loughery was the man. Kevin was a cool guy who always called me Tyrone. If I'm lucky, it was because I reminded him of movie star Tyrone Power. I never knew why he called me Tyrone and I don't know why I never asked.

The Nuggets were coached by another New York native, future Hall of Famer Larry Brown. Dynamic Rookie of the Year David Thompson and six-time ABA All-Star Dan Issel, a prolific scorer, were their two primary forces.

The Nets jumped out to a three-games-to-two lead in the series and headed back to the Nassau Coliseum for what would turn out to be the final game ever played in the ABA. It wasn't so much the game itself that stood out to me, but the fact that two brothers were announcing against each other.

I was calling the Nets game on television from courtside on the far-left side of the press table, adjacent to the Nets bench. My brother Al was doing the Nuggets TV play-by-play on the far-right side of the press table, next to the Nuggets bench.

The Nets found themselves trailing the Nuggets by a whopping twenty-two points late in the third quarter. Many of the fans in attendance and those watching on TV were probably thinking that the series was headed to a seventh and deciding game. David Thompson was brilliant, scoring forty-two points. Dan Issel looked unstoppable, with thirty points and twenty rebounds. All that said, the Nets had other ideas. Super John Williamson erupted for twenty-four of his twenty-eight points in the second half. Dr. J exploded for thirty-one points, nineteen rebounds, and five steals.

Did This Really Happen?

In a furious comeback, the Nets rallied to win 112-106, to capture the title. When the horn sounded to end the game, euphoric Nets fans stormed onto the court to celebrate the championship. Out of respect for the hometown announcer, wave after wave of deliriously happy Nets fans circumvented my end of the table. Down at the other end, they surged over the press table like a stampede of wild horses.

They terminated my brother's broadcast, ripping off his headset, severing wires, dragging his TV monitor to the floor, and obliterating his notes.

I saw Al standing on top of the table, where he sought refuge. There was nothing left but the tattered clothes he wore. He had a helpless look on his face that seemed to say, "What in the world just happened?" He never had a chance to sign off to the heartbroken Denver fans.

It was a different story on the victorious Nets side as I got to throw it to my broadcast partner, Bob Goldsholl, in the jubilant locker room where champagne was flowing. I felt compassion for my brother, but what a way to conclude my first year as television voice of the Nets.

That turned out to be the last time Al and I would announce against each other in the ABA, although we would go head-to-head many times in the NBA, as I also did with my other brother Marv.

The following season, the ABA merged with the NBA. The Nets, along with Denver, Indiana, and San Antonio, were absorbed into the NBA. As exciting as that was, the Nets paid an exorbitant price, losing Dr. J to the Philadelphia 76ers in exchange for $6 million. It just wasn't the same after that. Nevertheless, my only year in the ABA was the experience of a lifetime.

* * *

One of the funniest things that happened to me on the way to the broadcast booth took place with Phil Jackson, who was my color analyst on New Jersey Nets telecasts before he went into coaching. It happened one night before a game at the Meadowlands Arena. Our broadcast position was way upstairs in the hockey booth. Our on-camera position was at the edge of the booth, surrounded by fans. The games were televised on SportsChannel. For our on-air "uniforms," the station provided us with custom blue blazers with a red emblem sewn onto the left breast pocket.

A rare photo of Phil Jackson (left) announcing a New Jersey Nets game with me before he started his ring collection as the championship coach of the Bulls and Lakers.

On this particular evening, Phil and I were in our usual location, awaiting our cue to open the broadcast.

The producer's count started—ten, nine, eight—when suddenly a fan approached me, stuck his ticket in my face, and said, "Excuse me sir, can you show me to my seat?" He apparently mistook me for an usher, oblivious to the fact there were bright lights, a TV camera a few feet in front of me, and a microphone in my hand. I put my mic down and escorted him to his seat right next to the booth. When I returned and picked up the mic, Phil looked at me in astonishment.

Did This Really Happen?

"Hey," I said to Phil, "I was happy to oblige. Not only that . . . he was a good tipper."

The producer counted down three, two, one, and, without missing a beat, I said, "Hi everybody, this is Steve Albert, along with Phil Jackson, and welcome to New Jersey Nets basketball." Phil was laughing uncontrollably.

My Nets trading card. I could see where someone might mistake me for an usher.

* * *

It was opening night in 1994 at the Alamodome in San Antonio, Texas. I was doing the TV play-by-play for the Golden State Warriors. The hometown Spurs were pulling out all the stops. They wanted to bring the house down by setting off a massive fireworks display just before the Spurs were to be introduced to the capacity crowd. As it turned out, they almost did bring the house down. Literally.

It crossed my mind that the Alamodome, cavernous as it was, was an indoor facility. I said to my broadcast partner, Jim Barnett, "Indoor pyrotechnics. What could possibly go wrong?"

Before the introductions, the fireworks were set off—KABOOM! CRASH! BANG! Suddenly, sheets of water started cascading down from the upper deck, drenching fans and pouring onto the basketball court. It was an utter deluge. The fireworks had triggered a giant water cannon that was set to go off in the event of a fire. We found out that their sprinkler system worked. It worked really well. Thousands of gallons of water just exploded out of this cannon.

The arena was a disaster area. It looked like *The Poseidon Adventure*. Fans ran amuck, covering their heads with whatever they could find—game programs, hot dog wrappers, coats. I had never witnessed anything like it before at a sporting event. Warriors coach Don Nelson later remarked on our telecast that it looked like the "world's largest wet T-shirt contest."

As this fiasco was unfolding, Jim and I tried to make some sense of it on the air. When we went to a commercial, I hit the talkback button to our producer, Dan Becker, in the production truck.

I asked, "Does anybody back there have an umbrella?"

Dan said, "I'll check."

After a few seconds, he said, "Yes."

"Great, could somebody please bring it out to me?"

"Sure."

"And Dan, one more thing? When we come back after the commercial, can you please put us on camera?"

"No problem."

When we came back on the air, Jim and I were sitting at the broadcast table, talking while I held an umbrella over us. That shot made a lot of sports news highlights that night. The start of the game was delayed for nearly an hour.

Did This Really Happen?

Like I said, "Indoor pyrotechnics. What could possibly go wrong?"

My Warriors trading card, without an umbrella.

* * *

In the mid-1980s, my brother Al and I were both employed by WOR-TV (Channel 9) in New York, and later Secaucus, New Jersey, to anchor weeknight sports on their ten o'clock news broadcast. It was a unique setup. If not for a news director, Tom Petner, I'm not sure we could have pulled it off. Tom was an old-school newsman, yet he was not afraid to take chances. It didn't hurt that I was also surrounded by great co-workers and friends, like newswriters Bill Rubens and Budd Mishkin, and stage manager/associate director Steve Cohen.

Al and I basically alternated on the air. We worked out a schedule where one of us appeared each night. We kept sports producer Ira Piller on his toes.

A Funny Thing Happened on the Way to the Broadcast Booth

My brother Marv was at the time New York's preeminent sportscaster. He was the voice of the Knicks and the Rangers as well as sports anchor at WNBC-TV. Even though we were not in direct competition with Marv, since he was on at 6:00 and 11:00 p.m. and we were on at 10:00 p.m., WOR-TV was keen on the idea of having the two other Albert brothers on their news broadcast.

We weren't splitting the duties to lessen our workloads. The unique arrangement allowed us to continue our play-by-play obligations. At the time, I was announcing for the New Jersey Nets on television, while Al was the TV voice of the New Jersey Devils. We rarely appeared together at the same time on the newscast.

It did happen, however, most notably one night in 1986. One very messy night.

My brother Al (left) and I were all "choked up" for this WOR-TV (Channel 9) News publicity photo.

The New York Mets, whose games were televised on WOR-TV, had just won their second World Series in team history, beating the Boston Red Sox in seven games. It was their first championship since the Miracle Mets of 1969.

Did This Really Happen?

It was Al's turn to anchor the sports in the studio. We thought, if the Mets win, why not have me in their locker room, interviewing the jubilant players? It would be done via split screen, with Al on one side in the studio and me on the other side in the locker room.

The Mets were sitting on top of the baseball world, and there I was in the middle of the raucous celebration, standing on a platform getting ready to interview my fellow Lincoln High School alumnus, Lee Mazzilli. The locker room was bedlam, and champagne was erupting from bottles.

In the midst of the craziness, I was trying to watch the TV monitor and listen for Al's toss to me. Just as Al said, "Let's go to Steve in the victorious Mets' locker room," a shaving cream pie splatted all over my face. The hand that delivered the pie belonged to outfielder Kevin Mitchell. He had good aim and perfect timing, connecting precisely as I took the throw from Al.

The cream lathering my face was laced with talcum powder, so it not only blinded me but burned like the devil. Mazzilli, seeing that I was totally incapacitated, grabbed the microphone from me and said, "Al, I'll do the interview." Mazzilli proceeded to question me, inquiring how it felt to have a pie smashed in my face, cracking up as I struggled to answer.

I eventually regained my composure, wiped the stinging goop from my eyes, and continued the segment before throwing it back to Al in the comfortable, quiet, clean studio.

The drive home from Shea Stadium in Flushing, Queens, to Fort Lee, New Jersey, was one I'll never forget. My suit was soaked, my hair was a mess, and I smelled like a brewery.

Fortunately, I was not pulled over by the police—I would have had some serious explaining to do. I made it home in one piece and the following day sent my congratulations, along with a large dry-cleaning bill, to the world champions.

* * *

A Funny Thing Happened on the Way to the Broadcast Booth

New York's MSG Network aired a popular TV talk show called *Coors SportsNight* that was hosted by sportswriter-turned-sportscaster Dave Sims. The program's format was that of your standard late-night gab fest, with Dave sitting behind a desk next to a couch. The final component, of course, was the studio audience.

One night in 1987, the three Albert brothers were to be Dave's guests on the show. At the time, we were all doing sportscasting in one form or another in the New York area. In addition, we were all seen nationally, Marv on NBC, Al on *USA Tuesday Night Fights*, and yours truly on *Showtime Championship Boxing*.

Marv and I arrived at Madison Square Garden, where the show was done live, but we had to inform MSG president Bob Gutkowski that, unfortunately, Al couldn't make it. It came as a disappointment since they had promoted that the three of us would appear together, which was a rarity. The only previous time Marv, Al, and I had appeared together was at my bar mitzvah.

While we were waiting behind the curtain before going on, I had an idea. I said to Marv and Bob Gutkowski, "Why not sneak someone from the audience backstage and have the three of us walk out as the Albert brothers? The audience member would pose as Al, but let's make it someone who looks nothing like Al. It might be funny. What do we have to lose?"

They both thought about it for a second and said, "That's not bad."

During the next commercial, a staffer let Dave in on the joke. We peered out from behind the curtain, checking out the crowd to find our "double" for Al. I noticed a very strong candidate way in the back. He was a rather large, stocky gentleman with a mustache and wearing a lumberjack shirt, overalls, and a baseball cap. We all agreed that he was perfect.

Somebody from the staff went out to get him. Backstage, we introduced ourselves and explained the gag, telling him not to worry about saying anything—we would point out on camera that "Al" has laryngitis and can't talk. All he had to do was walk out with us, sit down on the couch, and nod his head. He told us he was all in. Fake Al was a great sport.

It was time for Dave to introduce us. "Now, ladies and gentlemen, making a rare TV appearance together, here they are, Marv, Al, and Steve Albert, the Albert brothers." The three of us walked out together. The place went nuts. It was a while before the laughter died down and Dave was able to talk again.

Marv (middle) and I on Coors *SportsNight,* hosted by Dave Sims (right). We chose an audience member to replace Al, who was unavailable.

Our backup Al did everything exactly right. Every time he nodded in response to a question from Dave, the crowd went berserk. Whenever the camera was on Fake Al, a caption identified him as Al Albert. Marv and I kept straight faces through the entire segment. Al's double was so good that the thought did cross our minds of trading him in for the real Al, or at least getting his number in case one of us couldn't make it to a family Thanksgiving.

A Funny Thing Happened on the Way to the Broadcast Booth

* * *

Now that I think of it, there was another time when Marv, Al and I appeared together that occurred after my bar mitzvah. It was on *The Tomorrow Show* with Tom Snyder on NBC. Prior to the taping, Tom greeted us in the hallway of 30 Rockefeller Center. I was nervous enough as it was, but then Tom told us that he had a bad cold and that we would have to carry the show. After introducing us on the air, Tom turned to me first and said, "Steve, what's Marv really like?"

I said, "Tom, people are always coming up to me, asking, 'What's Marv really like, how much money does Marv make, and when is Marv's next game?'"

After a short pause, I added, "And that was my father."

Tom let loose with his famous cackling laugh, which Dan Aykroyd had parodied many times on *Saturday Night Live*.

What a relief, and right out of the gate! From that moment on, my blood pressure normalized and I relaxed. We found out afterward that Tom enjoyed chatting with us so much that he bumped the other guests who were sitting in the greenroom. We were on for the entire hour. The other guests were an up-and-coming pair of comic illusionists known as Penn and Teller, who went on to become huge stars.

* * *

While in college, I was a summer intern at WNBC radio in New York. One night when I was assisting a talk show host named Long John Nebel, an in-studio guest was baseball personality and former big league catcher Bob Uecker. He was hilarious and had Long John laughing hysterically.

Uecker was nationally known for his frequent appearances on the *Tonight Show* starring Johnny Carson. He made up for a less-than-spectacular playing career with a self-deprecating sense of humor.

Did This Really Happen?

He captivated Carson with his deadpan style and dry wit. Carson jokingly referred to him as Mr. Baseball. On one show, Uecker described the easiest way to catch a knuckleball: "Wait until it stops rolling and just pick it up." With that quip, he brought down the house and Carson was on the floor.

Later, he became even more famous by flourishing in the movies, TV sitcoms and commercials.

In the early 1970s when I first started out in radio on WKYC, which soon became WWWE (a.k.a. 3WE) I hosted a pre-game show for the Cleveland Indians (now the Guardians). The Milwaukee Brewers came to town and I set out to interview none other than Bob Uecker, their lead play-by-play announcer.

I called the hotel where the Brewers were staying and asked the operator to connect me with Bob Uecker's room. When the person answered the phone and said hello, I thought I recognized Bob's voice. I introduced myself and asked if he had a few minutes to do a phone interview with me for the Indians pre-game show.

The voice on the other end suddenly switched to a Swedish accent, saying he was the hotel engineer and was in the room to repair the air conditioner.

I said, "Bob, this sounds like you." He insisted in the same inflection, "No, I'm the engineer and I'm in the room to fix the air conditioner. I'm the only one here."

This was before answering machines. In those days, when the phone rang, you picked it up. My theory is that when Bob heard my interview request, instead of turning me down, he pretended to be a Swedish engineer to spare my feelings.

Bottom line? The "engineer" hung up the phone and I did not get to interview Bob Uecker.

The years flew by, my career evolved and I never got around to resolving if that was actually Uecker I was talking to in the hotel room.

In 2025, Bob Uecker passed away at the age of 90.

It was an honor to be punked by him, if that indeed was him.

He was a lifetime .200 hitter who made it into the Baseball Hall of Fame . . . as a broadcaster. He was beloved in his native Wisconsin after fifty-four years behind the Brewers mic.

Untold Milwaukee fans who never even met Bob Uecker considered him a friend. And so did I.

* * *

Once at summer camp I lost in the finals of a tennis tournament to a kid with a broken arm. He had one arm in a cast. I kid you not.

I related that story to former major leaguer, author, actor, sportscaster, activist, and entrepreneur Jim Bouton, who developed the idea of personalized trading cards featuring people from all walks of life instead of professional athletes.

I enjoyed watching Jim when he pitched for the Yankees. His number was 56, which was unusually high back in the 1960s, and he threw the ball so hard, his cap would fly off his head. Bulldog, as he was known, developed a knuckleball that extended his career, and in 1970 he wrote the then-controversial bestseller *Ball Four*.

As I was walking to a tennis court with racket in hand one day, Jim approached me and asked if he could take my picture for one of his cards. When he requested a few background notes, I revealed the embarrassing summer camp episode. Here's what Jim wrote on the back of the card:

> At age 14, Steve lost the Camp Cayuga singles tennis championship to a kid with a broken arm. Steve has worked for the Nets, Crusaders, Cavaliers, Barons, and Generals, among others. He's bound for the *Guinness Book of Records* for most teams broadcasted for in one lifetime. Steve also has two brothers named Marv and Al.

* * *

Did This Really Happen?

Two guys in tuxedos walked into a Denny's restaurant in Bismarck, North Dakota. Sounds like the start of a joke, right? Only it was true, and I was one of the guys. The other was ring announcer Jimmy Lennon Jr.

It was after a *Showtime Championship Boxing* telecast. Local hero Virgil Hill had just defended his light heavyweight title in our main event, and following the broadcast Jimmy and I were looking for a place to grab a bite. It was slim pickings on this frigid winter night in Bismarck, but we finally found a Denny's. As you can imagine, we drew some strange looks. We seemed a tad overdressed.

We sat down at a table and as the waitress handed us the menus, we heard loud music and noise coming from another room. Moments later, a crowd of people burst into the dining room, trailed by a woman in a white wedding dress holding hands with a guy whom I assume was her new husband. Suddenly, our tuxes didn't seem so out of place. We should have tagged along with the wedding party to wherever they were headed.

A Funny Thing Happened on the Way to the Broadcast Booth

Dream Job

During my sophomore, junior, and senior years in high school, from 1965 through 1968, I had one of the coolest jobs a teenager could ever have. I was a ball boy for the New York Knicks. Tuesday and Saturday nights, when the Knicks played their home games, couldn't come fast enough.

After my last class on Tuesdays at Brooklyn's Lincoln High School, I would hop on the bus to the Brighton Beach station, then take the D train into Manhattan. My first season on the job, when the Knicks still played at the old Garden, I'd get off the train at the 50th Street stop. I would do my homework on the train and get home pretty late after work. I use the term *work*, but to me it was anything but because I loved doing it.

I can still remember the smells of Nedick's hot dog stand wafting with the cigarette and cigar smoke under the marquee of the old

A Funny Thing Happened on the Way to the Broadcast Booth

Madison Square Garden on Eighth Avenue between 49th and 50th Streets.

Big props to my brother Marv, then the Knicks radio announcer, who helped me get an interview with the team's business manager.

It was a pretty big responsibility for a fifteen-year-old kid, but my parents were very supportive. My mother even drove me to Schermerhorn Street in downtown Brooklyn to get my working papers.

This is the only photo I have as a ball boy for the New York Knicks, taken by legendary sports photographer and true gentleman George Kalinsky at the old Madison Square Garden.

The old Garden had a warm and intimate feel. I would get there hours before games, and one of the highlights was sometimes shooting around in the empty arena with Knicks TV director Chet Forte. Chet was a star basketball player at Columbia University who would become the first director of *Monday Night Football*. With his old-fashioned two-handed set shot, the ball almost always went in.

Then the players—Wilt Chamberlain, Bill Russell, Oscar Robertson, Jerry West—would start drifting onto the court, depending on the visiting teams. I would start doing my job, retrieving shots.

Standing on that familiar floor was mind blowing. Soon, the empty seats would be filled and the Garden would be buzzing. Out of public view, the locker rooms were small, especially by today's standards, but back then, there were fewer players, only one coach, and a single trainer—who was also the equipment manager and traveling secretary

The old Garden hosted doubleheaders back then. The nights were long but the tips were doubled.

By my third year with the team, the 1967–68 season, the new Garden at 34th Street above Penn Station was finally completed. The old Garden had become an old friend, and I was sorry to say goodbye. But it was nice to have a new tag team partner, a high school chum named Saul Mishaan who joined the ranks of the ball boys. Saul was an excellent baller himself who would later become a six-foot-three center for Brooklyn College.

Arriving at the new digs, I would head into the employees' entrance on 33rd Street between Seventh and Eighth Avenues and make my way up in the crowded service elevator crammed with Garden employees, food and beverage vendors, players, referees, sportswriters, and announcers. The smell of hot dogs, peanuts, and hot pretzels permeated the air. I remember how long the elevator ride seemed, as we usually stopped on every level. My excitement would build as we inched closer to the fifth floor, where the locker rooms and basketball court were.

Walking into the Knicks locker room never got old, thanks to the welcoming spirit of team trainer Danny Whelan, who was the trainer for the Pittsburgh Pirates when they won the World Series in 1960. Danny was a jovial white-haired San Franciscan who served in the Navy during World War II. He dubbed Walt Frazier with the nickname Clyde because he wore a hat similar to Clyde's in the movie *Bonnie and Clyde*. I was always greeted by Danny with an enthusiastic "Hello Stevie!" Then, I would change into my blue and orange Knicks jacket and head out to the floor. As I walked through the tunnel under the seats, I would hear the sounds of balls bouncing and sneakers squeaking as players warmed up.

I would take my position under the basket, fetch the "makes" and the "misses," and whip the balls back to the players, just like at the old Garden. The new surroundings were a lot plusher. It was magical, especially when Bill Bradley was out there. His shooting was absolute artistry.

I had a close-up view of the greatest basketball players in the world during three of the most enjoyable years of my youth. As a Knicks ball boy, I learned to appreciate the blood, sweat, and tears that went into being a professional athlete. The job also produced its share of unforgettable behind-the-scenes experiences.

* * *

During games, a Knicks fan favorite chose to sit at the very end of the bench, as far away from coach Red Holzman as possible. If he were any farther to the left, he'd have had to pay for his seat. I always parked myself right next to him, to his immediate right.

The game would be going on in front of us, and suddenly I would get an elbow jab to my ribs. "Get me a couple of dogs," the player would say. This request would occur almost every game.

There was a concession stand on our side of the arena, directly behind the stands in back of the Knicks bench. I would wait for a strategic moment, usually right after a timeout, so I could get back to the bench for the next timeout. I would dash over to the stand to buy two hot dogs.

Thankfully, there wasn't a long line when the game was in progress. I would get the franks, pay the vendor and hustle back around the stands to the Knicks bench. I would be relieved that another timeout hadn't been called while I was AWOL. I was the only ball boy on the bench, and if I wasn't there during a timeout to hand out water and towels to the players, I would need to do some explaining.

I would scurry back to the end of the bench without anybody else on the team noticing, plant myself next to the player, and discreetly slip him the two hot dogs. Bending his head down under a towel, he would use his right hand to cover his left hand, which held the hot dogs. He would quickly gulp down both dogs in four bites. Today, he could be a top contender at the annual July 4th Nathan's Famous International Hot Dog Eating Contest in Coney Island.

Of course, he didn't want fans to see what he was doing, and he most definitely didn't want Red Holzman to catch him in the act. He got away with it every time. Far be it from me to spill the beans now and reveal his identity.

* * *

Several years before he came to the Knicks as what many believed was the missing piece to their 1970 NBA championship season, Dave DeBusschere, a hardnosed forward known for his tenacious defense, was a player-coach for the Detroit Pistons. At six feet, six inches, DeBusschere had the combination of height, strength, and agility that makes 6-6 players such important assets. Can you even imagine the notion of player-coach today? The responsibilities would be ridiculously overwhelming. Debusschere did it at the age of twenty-four. Oh, and in his spare time, he pitched for the Chicago White Sox.

One night, the Pistons and their wunderkind came to the old Garden to play the Knicks. I was assigned to be the Pistons' ball boy. During this time, I was writing a column for my high school newspaper, the *Lincoln Log*, about my experiences as a Knicks ball boy. I would interview players with my portable tape recorder and transcribe the interviews at home on my typewriter.

I didn't want to miss this golden opportunity to chat with Dave DeBusschere about his extraordinary story. As he was about to change into his uniform, I approached the Pistons' young player-coach and asked if he could give me a few minutes for an interview. As if this guy didn't have enough to do, right? Now, some sniveling little shrimp comes up to him with an interview request.

Much to my surprise, he said, "Sure, no problem. Just give me a few minutes."

Moments later, after he was fully uniformed, Dave DeBusschere motioned for me to come over to the trainer's table, where the trainer taped the players' ankles. The table sat right in the middle of the Pistons locker room, which was the size of a walk-in closet.

Apparently, we were conducting the interview immediately before DeBusschere was to deliver his pregame pep talk. The players were sitting on chairs in front of their lockers, closely encircling the trainer's table in the cramped room.

The players were unaware that I was going to interview their coach and teammate, and they were waiting attentively for his pregame speech. DeBusschere gave them an at ease order so we could do the interview. However, the players thought they'd have a little fun and pulled their chairs even closer to us and leaned into the table to hear the conversation.

Have you ever had that feeling that all eyes are on you? Every one of the Detroit Pistons was watching my every move and waiting for me to open my mouth.

As the sweat began to drip down my brow and I slowly raised the microphone with my quivering hand, I somehow had the inspiration to look directly into Dave DeBusschere's eyes and say, "Now Dave, don't be nervous."

For a second, he had a look of amazement on his face and then he, along with the entire Pistons team, exploded spontaneously into loud laughter. It was the mother of all icebreakers, and I had somehow pulled it off.

I don't know what made me say those words or how I summoned up the nerve, but thank goodness I did. I had an entire NBA team eating out of my hands. After the laughter died down and the players

Dream Job

backed off, I conducted the interview, and Dave couldn't have been more gracious. It was a lesson that stayed with me forever. When you're up against the ropes, punch your way out . . . with humor.

* * *

One night before a Celtics-Knicks game at the old Madison Square Garden, I was doing my usual job of fielding loose basketballs from under the Celtics hoop. Some of the players took off their team warmup jackets and put them on the bench. Boston had unique fuzzy green fleece jackets with "Celtics" stitched on the front and a shamrock on the back. Players' names were attached with snaps above the shamrocks. The jackets were collector's items.

After the players completed their warmup shooting, I gathered all the jackets and took them to the locker room. It was early, and only a few fans were in the stands.

The Celtics trainer asked, "Where's Havlicek's jacket?"

John "Hondo" Havlicek, number 17, was an NBA great and a Boston icon. He was a thirteen-time All-Star and eight-time NBA champion who personified hustle and defense. An historic steal in game seven of the 1965 Eastern Conference finals cemented his legacy, as radio announcer Johnny Most's famous call of "Havlicek stole the ball" became Celtic folklore.

I hurried back out to the court and looked everywhere. I came up empty. Frantically, I ran back and examined every inch of the locker room. There was no sign of this prized jacket.

Minutes before the Celtics were to take the court for the opening tipoff, the trainer took me aside in the corridor just outside the team's locker room. He gave me a tongue-lashing like I had never heard before. The man had every reason to be upset. Fifteen-year-old kid or not, this was my responsibility.

Out of the corner of my eye, I could see Havlicek observing this scene from in front of his locker. When the Celtics started to run out to the Garden floor, the last man out was John Havlicek. He came up to me, put his arm around my shoulder, and said, "Don't worry, kid. I'll be all right without the jacket. I know you didn't take it." He couldn't have been nicer.

Many years later, Havlicek was appearing at an autograph show in New York. I was unable to be there, but a wonderful person named Cara Taback, who worked in public relations at Madison Square Garden and knew the story of the missing jacket, did attend.

Graciously, she brought an issue of *Sports Illustrated* with a nifty game action picture of Havlicek on the front cover. The headline story was entitled "Hero Havlicek of the Miracle Celtics."

She reminded John of the incident that had taken place at the old Garden and explained that that fifteen-year-old ball boy had grown up to be sportscaster Steve Albert.

He took the magazine and wrote the words, "To Steve, where is my jacket! I know you didn't take it. My best wishes, John Havlicek."

That particular *S.I.* is a special keepsake, and it will never, ever be among the missing, unlike John Havlicek's warmup jacket.

To this day, I have no idea what happened to it. This I do know—John Havlicek personified class.

* * *

On rare occasions, I would get to go on a road trip. For a teenage boy, that was about as good as it gets. They were trips that were close to New York, like Philadelphia or Boston, and they didn't require overnight stays, so it didn't cost the team a penny. The Knicks would bus it to that city for the game and after the game, bus it back to New York.

Not only did I get to sit on the team bench during games, now I got to sit on the team bus. It was fantastic.

My most vivid memory from those bus rides is that Bill Bradley was always reading a book. That was pretty unusual.

Bradley was an Ivy Leaguer, a Princeton grad, and a Rhodes Scholar, and it always seemed to me that while he loved basketball, playing hoops was something for him to do until he was ready for his next stage, which was politics. His nickname among teammates was "Mr. President." He sure came close, making it all the way to the Senate but falling short in his bid for the White House.

I have two Knicks ball boy road trip stories.

One took place in Boston. We arrived at the storied Boston Garden for a game against the Celtics that night. We all got out of the bus and, led by head coach Red Holzman and trainer Danny Whelan, made our way to the Knicks locker room.

When we arrived, the door was locked. Danny told me to go find somebody with the key. I ran back to the area where the bus had let us off. I explained to a security guard there that I was the Knicks ball boy, and I needed the key to open the door to the locker room. He tracked down the key, and I sprinted through the corridors of the Boston Garden back to the locker room.

When I got there, Knicks players were sitting on the hallway floor with their backs leaning against the wall. It was some sight. While some of the guys used the downtime for a catnap, others stared into oblivion, perhaps visualizing how the game might go.

Danny opened the door, and it must have been a hundred and twenty degrees in that room. Legend has it that Celtics general manager, Red Auerbach, would try almost anything to gain the advantage. This seemed to include making opponents wait outside the locker room so they would have less time to warm up on the court, and cranking the thermostat to make the Celtics' opponents sluggish. All you could do was shake your head.

* * *

On this other short excursion, I seem to recall that the players had brought their own uniforms for the game. One of the Knicks, who shall remain nameless, arrived in the locker room empty-handed. Coach Red Holzman was not amused.

A Funny Thing Happened on the Way to the Broadcast Booth

Team trainer Danny Whelan had spare jerseys on road trips, however the backs of the jerseys were blank.

Coach Holzman looked at me and said something to the effect of, "Hey kid, grab yourself a magic marker and write the player's name and number on the back of a jersey." Danny handed me a felt-tip pen and placed the jersey on the floor in the center of the Knicks locker room. I got down on my hands and knees and was about to start writing when I looked up and noticed that every Knicks player was staring at me. Each had a smirk on his face, some fighting back laughter, holding their hands over their mouths. They were enjoying this.

With my hand shaking from nerves, I started writing the player's name near the top of the jersey. Then, I wrote his number under the name. When I finished, it looked like a kidnaper's ransom note. The letters were all over the place and the number was tilted. Thankfully, the player who forgot his uniform took it in stride.

Yes, being a Knicks ball boy was quite an education. It was the kind you can't learn in a classroom and it sure made a kid from Brooklyn grow up fast. In addition, it helped me develop a variety of skills, like catering and waiting tables (learned from acquiring and serving hot dogs), as well as graphic design (a skill developed from applying a name and number to a jersey). In all seriousness, as the chapter title depicts, it positively was a dream job.

Name Dropping

During my high school years, I learned a lot about broadcasting while working as a gofer at WHN radio in Manhattan. I would fetch coffee and tea for the newsmen and disc jockeys. I worked in the music library, prepared weather and traffic updates, operated the switchboard (accidentally cutting off more than my share of calls), and even wrote features for some sports guy named Marv Albert.

Speaking of Marv, as far back as 1967, he was building followers. One of them was a thirteen-year-old aspiring sportscaster from Bayside, Queens, who was entering the eighth grade. This teenager had rounded up about fifty kids from his neighborhood to start a Marv Albert Fan Club. As the founder of that fan club, he would sometimes visit the WHN newsroom to interview my brother. Part of my job as an intern was to greet him in the lobby and walk him to

A Funny Thing Happened on the Way to the Broadcast Booth

meet Marv. His name? Howie Rose, who went on to become the longtime radio voice of the New York Mets.

* * *

One time, WHN news director, Mike Prelee, who resembled Lou Grant, the gruff but kindhearted news director on *The Mary Tyler Moore Show,* had no reporters available because they were all out on assignments. There was a big heist at the Waldorf-Astoria Hotel, and Zsa Zsa Gabor's jewelry had been stolen. Zsa Zsa was a glitzy, glamorous, bigger-than-life Hollywood actress who some might describe as famous for being famous.

Mike said to me, in true Lou Grant fashion, "Hey kid, grab a tape recorder and hurry over to the Waldorf and get some sound."

I said, "Yes sir," even though I had never done anything like this before.

I made my way over to the hotel, walked through its grandiose and ornate lobby, approached the front desk, and timidly asked the clerk, "Excuse me, sir, can you please tell me Zsa Zsa Gabor's room number?" Never in a million years would I have imagined I'd ever utter those words. Much to my surprise and amazement, he told me the room number.

When I got to the room, the door was slightly ajar. I knocked softly and gently nudged the door. I could see Zsa Zsa, elegantly attired, sitting on the couch and looking straight at me. She smiled and said in her instantly recognizable Hungarian accent, "Dahling, don't be bashful. Come on in." Ordinarily, if Zsa Zsa Gabor had said to me, "Dahling, don't be bashful. Come on in," my heart would have skipped a beat, but seeing a swarm of reporters and TV cameras surrounding her, it kind of spoiled the mood, if you know what I mean.

I stuck my microphone into the crush of hands and mics in front of her face. My hand was the only one shaking, but I managed to get some good sound from Zsa Zsa, and the news director was pleased.

If there's one thing I learned from those early years in radio, it's to never say no to any request. Don't ever turn down a job.

* * *

As a college student at Kent State, I worked at the campus radio station, WKSU. The station manager once asked me to run over to the athletic center.

I immediately responded, "Who's playing?"

He said, "Johnny Mathis."

"Johnny Mathis, the singer? Who's he playing?"

"Real funny. We need you to go there and interview Johnny Mathis."

I was curious. "Why do you want me to interview Johnny Mathis? I'm in sports."

"Because there's nobody else around."

I grabbed a tape recorder and off I went. Mathis was performing at the university that night. On my way to the gym, I wondered, "What am I going to ask him?" He was one of the greatest pop music artists in the world, with hit songs like "It's Not for Me to Say," "Chances Are," and "Wonderful, Wonderful." Beyond that, I didn't know anything about him.

Just then, I remembered reading somewhere that Johnny Mathis had been a track star in his school days. I thought, "It might be a little unorthodox, but it's worth a shot, or it could be a total disaster."

I arrived at his dressing room and introduced myself. We sat down, I started the tape recorder, and right off the bat, I asked him about his track and field days. His face lit up. I could tell by his smile that he couldn't believe I knew about that, and he seemed genuinely pleased to talk about this subject. "It's Not for Me to Say," but "Chances Are," it's "Wonderful, Wonderful" that I was asked to interview Johnny Mathis.

* * *

A Funny Thing Happened on the Way to the Broadcast Booth

When I worked at WWWE radio in Cleveland, renowned country singer-songwriter Glen Campbell came to town to perform, and he made a publicity stop at the radio station. There was nobody around to interview him, so guess who was appointed?

The station manager said, "Hey Steve, if you're not doing anything right now, can you go to the studio and interview Glen Campbell?"

We're talking about the man who recorded megahits like "Gentle on My Mind," "By the Time I Get to Phoenix," "Wichita Lineman," and "Galveston." No pressure, right? I was still pretty wet behind the ears, but I remembered the experience in college with Johnny Mathis. The only problem was, I never saw anything about Glen Campbell being a track star.

I decided to take a different tack: honesty. When Glen showed up, I explained to him that I was a sportscaster, primarily the hockey play-by-play announcer for the station, and that there was no one else available to do the interview. He said he completely understood, and I think he appreciated my frankness. Glen gladly talked about his career, and he couldn't have been friendlier. He made me look good. I had always liked Glen Campbell the musician, but after that encounter, I was a fan for life of Glen Campbell the person.

* * *

When I arrived at Kent State, I couldn't wait to get on the air at the radio station. I was fortunate to have some experience in high school working behind the scenes as an intern for a major radio station in New York, but I had no on-air experience.

One opportunity came the summer after my freshman year when I returned home to Brooklyn. I had contacted the New York Yankees public relations director and scored a one-on-one interview with Kent State's Golden Boy, Thurman Munson, the greatest baseball player in the school's history. The Canton, Ohio, product was just a rookie catcher at the time, but he was already projected to be a star.

Name Dropping

He exceeded expectations, eventually becoming Rookie of the Year, Most Valuable Player, seven-time All-Star, two-time World Series Champion, and the Yankees' first team captain since Lou Gehrig, before his untimely death in a plane crash at the age of thirty-two.

As Thurman's remarkable career unfolded, he would develop a reputation as being surly toward the media. No matter how good you are, playing under the New York microscope is a major challenge for any athlete. Some cope with it better than others, but the intense scrutiny can take its toll on even the coolest customer.

When I met him, Thurman Munson was a fresh-faced kid, only a year or so out of Kent State, and he seemed honestly thrilled to converse with a fellow Flash. (Kent State's nickname is the Golden Flashes.) I still remember his smile as we sat down next to each other in the Yankees dugout. He proudly wore his Yankee pinstripes, the number 15 on his back, and he couldn't have been more forthcoming once we started rolling. I recall it was about a fifteen-minute interview, and when the new school year started, WKSU couldn't wait to put it on the air. I only wish I still had the tape.

The interview was a home run with everybody at the radio station, and it gave me a healthy dose of self-assurance. Still, I had a lot to learn and, boy, there were times when I floundered, in spite of the early exposure I had to the business. I learned that observing the craft is one thing. Doing it is another.

* * *

I never thought I would get to see Muhammad Ali fight in person, let alone interview him. While I was broadcasting hockey in Cleveland, guess who came to town to fight? That's right, the Greatest himself. It was March 24, 1975, and Ali had a date with Chuck Wepner, aka the Bayonne Bleeder. The match took place at the Richfield Coliseum, where I was calling games at the time for the Cleveland Crusaders.

A Funny Thing Happened on the Way to the Broadcast Booth

It was Ali's first fight after the Rumble in the Jungle, when Ali KO'd George Foreman in the eighth round to become the heavyweight champion of the world for the second time. That fight took place in Kinshasa, Zaire, a long way from the Cleveland suburb of Richfield, Ohio. Nobody was giving Wepner much of a chance.

In a shocking moment, Ali was dropped in the ninth round. It was a controversial knockdown, as Ali accused the underdog of stepping on his foot. Wepner of course claimed otherwise. It was only the fourth time in Ali's career that he had been on the canvas. Wepner had guts and stamina and managed to last into the fifteenth round before being knocked out.

It was a night to remember, and I couldn't believe I was fortunate enough to be there. Another spectator in the crowd that night was a young actor named Sylvester Stallone. That fight was his inspiration for *Rocky*.

Fast forward a few years. I was a sports anchor at WCBS-TV in New York, and prior to Muhammad Ali's fight against Ernie Shavers at Madison Square Garden, I got to do a face-to-face interview with the champ. After my first question, he looked at me with a smirk and said, "You ain't as dumb as you look." We both chuckled, and he proceeded to give me good, thoughtful answers. His opening line was just his way of being playful and funny. It's a good thing I laughed, or I might have become the Brooklyn Bleeder.

* * *

When I was working at WABC radio, morning drive time host Alan Colmes couldn't have been more generous. He would invite me to participate in segments beyond my sports reports. Afterward, I would hustle back to the newsroom, knock out another sportscast on the typewriter, then rush back to the studio.

One time he had someone on his show I truly admired, Fred Rogers, better known as Mister Rogers, host of the children's TV series *Mister Rogers' Neighborhood*. After I did my sports update,

Name Dropping

Alan asked me to join him for the interview with Mister Rogers, who happened to mention that he was from Latrobe, Pennsylvania. I remembered that famed golfer Arnold Palmer was from the same town, so I asked him if he knew Arnold and whether he ever played golf with him. Fred lit up with a big grin, confirmed that he did, and talked at some length about golfing with Palmer. It seemed like a welcome departure for him. I guess he seldom discussed the subject.

You know how sometimes you're reluctant to meet a celebrity you admire for fear of being disappointed? Mister Rogers blew that notion to smithereens.

* * *

One morning when I was a sports anchor at WCBS-TV in New York, I was assigned to go with a camera crew to a restaurant and bar on Central Park South in Manhattan. Not just any restaurant and bar, it belonged to former Yankee great Mickey Mantle.

The Mick wanted some publicity for his new establishment, which was still under construction. He brought along a couple of his friends—pinstripe legends Billy Martin and Whitey Ford.

All three of them, not just Mickey, wanted to participate in the on-camera interview. That was fine by me. Mickey was standing to my immediate left, Billy and Whitey on my right.

While talking with Billy and Whitey, I felt a hand pinch my rear end. The hand belonged to Mickey Mantle, who was having a little fun at my expense. Mickey did not let up as I continued moderating the dialogue. Billy and Whitey had no idea what was going on behind us.

After we finished, Mickey took me aside, looked me straight in the eyes, and said, "Steve, you knew what I was doing during the interview, yet you didn't even flinch. You're a true pro."

I was not a Yankee fan as a kid, but I revered Mickey Mantle. Here was the Mick, telling me to my face, "You're a true pro." I felt like I had come off the bench to hit a walk-off homer. Talk about a "pinch" hit.

* * *

Every few months, I go to one of the great eateries in New York City called Barney Greengrass, home to the best potato latkes on earth. I go there not only for the delicious cuisine, but to break bread with a bunch of very talented people, many of whom tell fabulous jokes, some of which cannot be repeated in a G-rated book.

The organizer is an old friend and colleague of mine named Budd Mishkin. Budd is a broadcast journalist who used to host a show called *One on 1* on NY1, the 24-hour news and information channel in the Big Apple. Through his show, Budd developed bonds with many interesting personalities he interviewed from the acting, music, broadcasting, and literary industries who reside in the New York area. He thought it would be fun to get as many of these folks together for good food and scintillating conversation. He was right. We call it the Barney Greengrass Group. The regulars include actors Richard Kind and Peter Riegert, actor and musician Ruben Blades, musicians Will Lee, John Pizzarelli, and Neal Shulman, music producer Russ Titelman, writer/songwriter Joe Cosgriff, sound technician/producer Mark Solomon, and me. In addition, there have been cameo appearances by other creative types such as comedy writer Alan Zweibel, composer Michael Giacchino, writer/author David Margolick, humorist/author Calvin Trillin, musician Marc Cohn, and producer Matt Ginsburg.

During the COVID pandemic, the Barney Greengrass Group did not miss a beat and got together on Zoom. The conversation was still scintillating. The latkes? Not so much.

* * *

Name Dropping

You never know who's out there watching you on television.

As my Showtime broadcast partner Bobby Czyz and I were settling in to our seats on a flight from New York to Los Angeles to do a boxing telecast, we received a visit from another passenger. It was none other than the sultry-voiced star of stage, screen and television Suzanne Pleshette, famous for her role as Emily Hartley on *The Bob Newhart Show*.

She came over to introduce herself and explained that she was a big boxing fan who had watched many of our fight shows on TV. I wasn't sure who was more excited, Suzanne or us?

After chatting for a while, Suzanne asked Bobby and me to walk over to the other side of the plane to say hello to her husband, TV and film actor Tom Poston. Tom was on both of Bob Newhart's sitcoms, but he's best known for playing the handyman on Newhart. I was a huge fan of his as a kid, recalling his time on *The Steve Allen Show*. Tom was in the hilarious "Man on the Street" segments along with Don Knotts, Bill Dana, Louie Nye, Dayton Allen and Pat Harrington Jr. Tom played the man who could never remember his name.

Bobby and I were thrilled to meet both stars and went back to our seats. I've had other show biz personalities say hi to me on airplanes like LL Cool J and Cedric the Entertainer. I remember when James Caan and Tony Orlando, during separate fight shows, tapped me on the shoulder to say hello while I was on the air. Suzanne Pleshette, however, was an unexpected fan. As I said, you never know who's watching.

* * *

Once, WABC radio host Alan Colmes had invited a gifted comedian and voice-over actor named Gary Yudman to do a phone bit on the show. Gary was to play the role of Vinko Bogataj.

Vinko Bogataj was a ski jumper from the former Yugoslavia who was featured every week on the opening of ABC's *Wide World of*

Sports, in which a voice-over spoke the catchphrase "the thrill of victory and the agony of defeat."

During the event featured in the show opening, Bogataj was representing his country in a ski competition in West Germany. The conditions were not ideal, and poor Vinko lost his balance and went out of control, violently careening down the course, ultimately crashing into a fence near spectators, all of which was caught on camera. Vinko Bogataj became the poster child for the agony of defeat as TV viewers watched him rumble down that mountain every week.

Fortunately, it looked a lot worse than it was, and Vinko suffered only a mild concussion and a broken ankle.

Alan asked me to participate in the spoof with Gary. In a perfect Eastern European accent, Gary, as Vinko, explained that he was currently working as a forklift operator in his native Yugoslavia.

As part of the parody, I asked him if he could reenact the experience of hurtling down the hill in the horrifying clip we saw every Saturday on *Wide World of Sports*.

Without hesitation, Gary said in the Slav accent, "Sure, of course. Here goes."

I'm not doing this justice, but it went something like this: "Oh, oh, oh, oh! Oh my god, oh my god! Look out, look out!"

His voice getting louder and more dramatic, he continued, "I'm falling, I'm tumbling! Hey, get out of my way! Oy, yoy, yoy! I can't believe this! Watch out for that bump! Ouch, ouch, ouch! Ooh that hurts! Oh boy, oh boy! Holy crap!"

On and on he went. What made that so impressive is that Gary did not know I was going to ask him that. He improvised it on the spot, and it was hilarious, comedy gold. We couldn't stop laughing. It went over very well, and I'm so happy I kept the cassette tape of that. Now, all I have to do is find a cassette deck so I can play it.

* * *

One time, just prior to announcing a Phoenix Suns game against the Lakers in Los Angeles, I happened to point out to our stage manager, John "JR" Reynolds, that one of my all-time favorite sports movies was *Hoosiers*. I even had a ritual of watching the film before every NBA season for motivation. I can never get enough of hearing the fictional Jimmy Chitwood's words—"I'll make it"—to Coach Norman Dale (played by Gene Hackman) during the final time-out of the championship basketball game. Jimmy made the last-second shot to give small-town Hickory High School the 1952 Indiana state title.

I had mentioned to JR that I wondered what happened to the *Hoosiers* actor who portrayed Jimmy Chitwood. Within a minute, JR handed me his cell phone with Maris Valainis (the actor who played Jimmy Chitwood) on the other end. Maris was a friend of JR's. We had a brief chat. I learned that Maris had moved on from acting, did some motivational speaking, and got into business consulting.

Who needs to watch *Hoosiers* for motivation when I can personally talk to "Jimmy Chitwood" instead?

A Funny Thing Happened on the Way to the Broadcast Booth

Living Through History

May 4, 1970, the day of the Kent State shootings, was a Monday, but things had really begun to heat up over the previous weekend.

In my sophomore year at Kent State, Vietnam had gripped the student body and when President Richard Nixon escalated the war by invading Cambodia, things finally boiled over. Storefront windows in downtown Kent were broken. Bottles were thrown at the local police. Tear gas was used to disperse the crowd. The ROTC building was set ablaze. It was an extremely tense, jittery time on the Kent State University campus. The normally low-key school had suddenly changed its vibe.

In response, Ohio Governor James Rhodes had dispatched the National Guard to occupy the campus on Saturday night, May 2. Schoolwork, however, went on and I needed to get a project done.

That Saturday night, I had to go to the library to finish a term paper for a course in television. I knew I was in for a long night, but I had no idea how frightfully it was going to end. After wrapping things up in the library, I gathered my books and papers and headed for the door. I had been there for hours, and when I walked outside it was pitch black and eerily silent.

As I started to walk to my dorm, two soldiers ran toward me with their bayonets pointed at me. They yelled, "Halt!" They scared the daylights out of me. Holding books under both arms, I didn't move a muscle.

One of them asked, "Where are you going?"

"I'm going back to my dorm. I was in the library doing a term paper."

The soldier continued, "Don't you know there's a curfew?"

I apologized, saying I was so involved in my work I must have lost track of time.

He stared at me for a few seconds before proclaiming, "We'll escort you back to your dorm."

So, they did, one on each side of me. Not a word was said from start to finish. All I could hear was the sound of their boots on the ground and the sound of crickets as we made our way to my safe haven. When we arrived at the entrance to my dorm, I said, "We're here," and off they went. This military escort experience gave me a lot to think about that late Saturday night.

The next day, Sunday, May 3, I was still pondering this interaction as I looked outside from my dormitory. I snapped out of it and saw that it must have rained overnight. The grounds were wet and muddy. Some students, apparently needing to let off some steam, started to roll around in the mud and engage in mud fights. As I watched the action from the large window in a hallway several floors up, I could see it was all harmless fun. Just kids doing what kids do, particularly after a long, stressful week of classes. I could make out the sounds of laughter, and I could see smiling faces. I remember it brought a smile to my face as well. However, word of this "unusual" activity in our area must have spread to another part of the campus, as almost out of nowhere a battalion of soldiers came marching toward the dorm.

The students rollicking in the mud could not see them approaching, but I saw them closing in from my upstairs perch. Suddenly, I saw someone run out from the dorm lobby below toward the troops, frantically waving his arms, trying to stop them from coming closer. I assume it was one of the dormitory graduate assistants.

When that person reached the lead officer, I saw him start talking. I don't know what he was saying, but the officer listened intently. My heart was pounding. A couple of minutes went by, then all at once, the officer instructed the soldiers to turn around. After an abrupt about-face, they started to march away. Whatever that person said, it worked, and I breathed a sigh of relief. I don't want to think about what might have happened had that alert person not defused the situation.

Monday morning, I went to my 11:00 a.m. class in child psychology, as I did every Monday, having no idea that from this day forward, the date of May 4 would be etched forever in my memory. I want to make clear that while I was on the campus that day, I was not an eyewitness to the shootings.

A student demonstration had been scheduled for noon near Taylor Hall, the journalism and architecture building. Students were protesting the intensification of the war and the National Guard's occupancy on campus. My class was just minutes by foot from the rally.

I remember that when I registered for this class, I grimaced when I saw that it met in two-hour sessions. Later, I realized that that extra hour may have affected the course of my life. Had it been a conventional one-hour class, I probably would have been walking back across campus toward my dorm in the direction of the shootings at the time they occurred. I would have seen the students gathering and perhaps out of curiosity gotten closer to the crowd. Who knows what would have happened if I was there?

In the second hour of class, shortly after noon, the teacher was showing an instructional film in which a baby was crying loudly. Over the din of the wailing infant, my classmates and I heard sirens blaring outside the building. We couldn't tell if they were ambulances, fire trucks, or police cars, but we knew that something was wrong.

I can't recall if the class was dismissed or we just ran out of the classroom on our own. Once outside, we saw other students running aimlessly. I sprinted as fast as I could toward my dorm. When I reached the lobby, a female voice was screaming over the public address system, "Go up to your rooms, grab anything you can, and get the hell off the campus!" She repeated, "Get the hell off the campus!"

To this day, I've never forgotten those words reverberating through the lobby or the urgency in her voice.

I raced up to my room, where I found my roommates, Howie, Barry, and Nick. I'm not sure we said anything. We hurriedly went through our dresser drawers and grabbed whatever we could. I randomly stuffed articles of clothing into my little satchel, then threw on my Kent State jacket. The four of us rushed downstairs and ran outside.

The road leading off campus was overflowing with students and overrun by vehicles in bumper-to-bumper traffic, and there was a cacophony of honking horns. People were frantically trying to exit the campus. We weren't sure what we were running from. We had heard there was gunfire, but we had no idea about the magnitude of the day's events. As we found out later, the panic to flee the school grounds was because people were not certain that the shooting was over. Remember, this was long before the age of cell phones, social media, and instantly available information. All we knew was that something had happened at that demonstration.

The four of us managed to jump into some stranger's convertible, and we hitched a ride to Akron, Ohio, to Nick's family home. Nick then drove Howie, Barry, and me to Akron-Canton Airport. Like me, Howie and Barry were from New York. Fellow students were wildly trying to get on planes. I wanted to call my parents in Brooklyn and tell them not to worry, but the pay phones were thronged with students who had the same idea. The lines to purchase a plane ticket were enormous.

I could only imagine what my parents were going through, not knowing if their son was safe.

I finally managed to get my ticket and board the plane. While I remember most of my personal experiences on that distressing day, the flight is for some reason somewhat of a blur. Maybe that's a good thing. It may mean that it was uneventful. I just recall that it was quiet. Perhaps we were all in shock or simply worn out, or both.

We landed at Newark Airport in New Jersey, where I got on a bus to Manhattan, then jumped on the subway to Brooklyn. That was followed by another bus ride into Manhattan Beach. I recall other passengers looking at me kind of strangely on the train and buses. Then I remembered that I was wearing my Kent State jacket.

I still didn't have a clear picture of exactly what had happened earlier in the day back in Ohio. I had heard bits and pieces of news, that there were possible fatalities, but nothing official.

During my trip home, I still had been unable to reach my parents. In what seemed like the blink of an eye, here I was back in noisy, gritty New York. My life seemed upside down. That morning, I had been sitting in a classroom on the rural campus of Kent State University, and only hours later, here I was, in the living room of my house in Brooklyn under circumstances I could never have imagined. The whole day was like a weird dream.

I learned later that my brother Marv had desperately been trying all day to reach me and was scouring the newswires at his radio station for information so he could let my parents know what was going on. The events of the day were still vague and unconfirmed, and concerns intensified when it was rumored that a student from New York had been shot and killed.

I walked into our house on Kensington Street just before seven o'clock the evening of May 4. My folks were getting ready for dinner. They were greatly relieved to see me, but like me, they had yet to learn the true gravity of the situation. Then we all sat down to watch the *CBS Evening News* with Walter Cronkite. Kent State was the lead story. For the first time, I saw images of the armed soldiers marching toward the unarmed students. I finally learned the details of what had happened that day. Four students were killed. Nine others were wounded.

* * *

My story takes a turn here. I was still trying to absorb what had happened when, the very next day, out of the blue, I received a phone call from New York Knicks trainer Danny Whelan, who knew that I was attending Kent State.

As I chronicled earlier, I had been a New York Knicks ball boy during my last three years of high school. Danny had called to invite me to sit on the Knicks bench as an honorary ball boy at Madison Square Garden for game seven of the NBA championship against the Los Angeles Lakers on May 8. I thanked Danny profusely for the opportunity. I scrambled to find my blue and orange Knicks jacket and counted the hours.

That game turned out to be one of the most memorable events in sports history. It was a night that New York sports fans and even nonfans will remember forever. Willis Reed, the Knicks captain and heart of the team, unlikely to play because of a severe thigh injury, surprised and electrified everyone when he hobbled onto the Garden floor to a deafening roar from the stunned sellout crowd.

I have to admit I had an inkling that Willis would at least try to play. I was in the locker room before the game, watching up close as he was injected in the hip with the painkiller Carbocaine by the team doctor, with a rather formidable syringe, I might add. It was the scariest looking needle I had ever seen. Sometimes I still can't believe I was behind the scenes to see this taking place.

Moments later, I was standing on the court near the Knicks bench when Willis emerged from the tunnel. The Garden was rocking, and to find myself in the middle of this magical moment was an out-of-body experience. Willis, who could barely walk, dragged his leg onto the floor. When the fans saw him, they exploded.

Up in the broadcast booth, my brother Marv, the Knicks radio announcer, uttered the words "Here comes Willis!" When Willis Reed hit his first warmup shot, the crowd noise was so earsplitting, it felt as if the building was shaking. Then Willis hit another warmup shot, and the decibel level went up still further. If you didn't have goose bumps, you weren't human.

The Lakers, warming up on the other side of the court, suddenly stopped what they were doing. Every player in purple and gold turned around, each transfixed by Willis Reed.

I stared into the eyes of Wilt Chamberlain. Then I looked closely at Jerry West. Both were standing just a few feet from me. I knew at that moment that the game was over, that the Lakers were totally psyched out, that the Knicks were going to win their first championship.

The injection enabled Willis to start the game and play twenty-seven minutes. Basically, on one leg, he hit the Knicks' first two shots of the game, sending the crowd into a frenzy. They would turn out to be his only points of the night. Defensively, he shut down Wilt Chamberlain, who'd had forty-five points and twenty-seven rebounds in game six. The Knicks took a 69-42 half-time lead into the locker room. After that, Walt "Clyde" Frazier grabbed the reins and finished with a commanding thirty-six points and nineteen assists.

The Knicks won, 113-99, for their first-ever NBA championship. In the limited time Willis Reed was on the floor, he had done his job. He inspired the Knicks to victory. After the game, Howard Cosell told Willis on national TV, "You exemplify the very best that the human spirit can offer."

In the final minutes of the game, which was well in hand, Danny instructed me to gather up all the Knicks warmups. He knew that bedlam would reign at the sound of the buzzer and the Knicks gear would be scarfed up by the fans. As the clock dwindled down, I picked up everything and made my way around the edge of the court and dropped it all off in the Knicks locker room. I could hear the crowd going wild and as I stood by the locker room entrance, one by one, the players came in—Walt Frazier, Dave DeBusschere, Bill Bradley, Dick Barnett, and, of course, Willis Reed. In the beautifully-written book *When the Garden Was Eden*, author Harvey Araton kindly included my Kent State/Knicks ball boy adventure. He captured it perfectly.

The whole scenario was difficult to comprehend. In just four days, I went from the Kent State campus, scene of one of the most tragic events in our nation's history, to what was arguably the most glorious and celebrated night in New York sports history, one of the most iconic of all time. There was only one word to describe it: surreal.

A few weeks later, after we completed take-home exams, Howie's father drove Howie and me back to Kent State to pick up the rest of our belongings. The campus was like a ghost town. The grounds, usually so green, vibrant, and well-manicured, looked uncharacteristically grim. Left unattended, everything was stark and dreary. We seemed to be in a black-and-white movie.

We went to our dormitory, packed everything up, then made the long journey back to New York.

* * *

In 2019, a year before the 50th anniversary of the shootings, I returned to Kent State. I visited the May 4 Memorial Museum and toured the grounds where the shootings occurred. Memories of that day came flooding back.

During this trip, I also participated in the Kent State Shootings Oral History Project, organized by the KSU Library, and provided a narrative of my experiences of the May 4 event.

The shootings by American soldiers at American students were so shocking it triggered a nationwide student strike that forced hundreds of colleges and universities to close. Every year on the anniversary of the massacre, Kent State commemorates the event. What happened on that horrible day in 1970 should never be forgotten.

A Funny Thing Happened on the Way to the Broadcast Booth

Starting Kent State Hockey

I went to college to start a hockey team. Implausible? Ridiculous? Who goes to college for that reason? To me, it made total sense.

Other schools had hockey programs, but most had established hockey announcers. I faced the possibility of having to wait in the wings as an understudy and never being given the opportunity to announce. I thought if I started my own team, I could appoint myself the announcer. It was to me the most expedient way to get experience doing hockey play-by-play, so as to help me with my ultimate goal of announcing professional hockey.

All I had to do was find a school that had a broadcasting curriculum and didn't have a hockey team. That was Kent State University.

When I was accepted into Kent State and started school, I wasn't sure how I was going to implement my plan. As the school had no hockey team, it had no hockey rink, no hockey players and no hockey coach. It was going to be a challenge.

A Funny Thing Happened on the Way to the Broadcast Booth

While I figured out what to do about starting a hockey team, my primary objective while in college was to get as much broadcasting experience as possible. When I arrived on campus, the first thing I did was head to the student radio station, WKSU, to apply for a position. I got a job and started doing sports reports on the radio and even hosted a classical music show. Later on, I did sports reports on WKSU-TV, the campus television station.

Over the next two years, I grabbed as many college broadcasting jobs as I could, all the while trying to think about how to get a hockey team started. I did play-by-play of freshman basketball, varsity baseball, and wrestling. I even did public address announcing for gymnastics.

I wanted to announce the varsity basketball and football games, but the university was using professional announcers. I thought this unfairly deprived students of valuable broadcasting experience. Undeterred, I would bring my tape recorder to games and do practice play-by-play.

Despite my strong desire, I still could not figure out how to get a hockey team started so I could also announce hockey.

Then the broadcasting gods smiled on me.

When I returned to Kent State for my junior year, my eagerness to start a hockey team received a major boost. Construction of an ice arena had been completed on campus.

Inside it looked like a Swiss ski chalet. A lounge with a large fireplace separated the two rinks, one a figure skating rink and the other a hockey arena with a seating capacity of about fifteen hundred.

When I opened the door to the arena for the first time and walked in, I was like a kid in a candy store. It even had a broadcast booth.

I ran up to the booth and looked down onto the ice. I started to imagine a jam-packed house with fans wildly cheering on Kent State's first hockey team. I could hear the crowd. I could see the players busting down the ice, streaking toward the opposing goal. I'm upstairs doing play-by-play—"He shoots, he scores!" I was in hockey heaven and supercharged, and I couldn't wait to spring into action.

When I finally came back down to earth, I realized that step number one was to find a coach. I'd heard that the school had hired a former defenseman from Boston University, a native of Hamilton, Ontario, Canada, named Don Lumley, to teach ice-skating. Don's BU team made it to the NCAA finals in 1967, only to lose to Cornell and future Hockey Hall of Fame goaltender Ken Dryden.

While I was gung ho to get this enterprise off the ground, the thought of approaching a stranger to make a pitch caused the butterflies in my stomach to engage in gastric combat.

Eventually, I worked up the courage to introduce myself to Don after he finished teaching a skating class. I explained my mission and asked if he would be interested in being the coach. I don't recall his exact words, but following our conversation, I came away thinking that he wasn't totally enthralled with the idea.

After I found the guts to badger him a few more times, Don finally relented and said that if I could round up enough students for a tryout, he would grab a whistle, head over to the hockey rink, and check things out. To this day, I don't think he thought that I could rustle up two hockey lines, let alone an entire roster.

I printed flyers to publicize tryouts for the first-ever Kent State ice hockey team. I put them up everywhere on campus in the next few days, probably hitting every dormitory, classroom, cafeteria, bulletin board, car windshield, lamp post, and tree, along with the student union, the gym, and men's rooms. I even snuck into women's bathrooms to post announcements.

"Bring your own uniforms, equipment, and hockey sticks," the flyers said. "We'll provide the pucks." Remember, this is well before the internet, Facebook, and X. We communicated the old-fashioned way—through posters, newspaper stories, ads, telephone, and, yes, by good old word of mouth.

When tryout day arrived, I walked into the hockey arena and could not believe my eyes. It was a great turnout. I walked over to the figure skating rink where Don Lumley was standing and said, "Coach, I think you better come with me . . . and, oh yeah, grab a whistle."

By my estimation, about seventy-five students came out. Many of them were wearing ragtag team jerseys and sweaters you'd see in street hockey games. Some were decked out in their old high school uniforms, and some were wearing figure skates. They looked like hockey's rendition of the Bad News Bears. To me, though, they were a beautiful sight.

Don hopped onto the ice, and it was the dawn of Kent State hockey.

It took several days, but Coach Lumley eventually whittled the group down, and when the ice shavings settled, Kent State had its first hockey team.

Once Don started running that open tryout, I could see that he was a born coach and an excellent organizer. I instantly dubbed him Kent State's Mr. Hockey, a nod to the great Gordie Howe.

Guess who was his first cut? That's right. The guy who started the whole dang thing. I tried out, thinking I could play and announce. I was hoping that some of my brother Al's skills had rubbed off on me. I soon found out that roller hockey on the streets of Brooklyn wasn't quite the same as hockey on the ice at Kent State.

I'll always remember how kind and compassionate Don was. He broke it to me gently. I was in the locker room getting dressed when he came over to me and said, "Excuse me, no visitors allowed."

Seriously, it went more like, "Steve, you be our president and announce the games." It was a nice way of saying, "Steve, you stink." I understood, and after a while, my bruised ego didn't feel as bad as my bruised bones from Don's rigorous workouts. I figured it would be a lot easier on my body up in the broadcast booth, so I willingly took the coach's suggestion. After all, the main reason I started this whole thing in the first place was to do the play-by-play—which is where I ran into my first snag.

When I met with the professor who managed WKSU, the campus radio station, about putting the hockey games on the air, the conversation did not go according to my plan. He had no interest in broadcasting the games.

His focus was on classical music, not sports. It was a punch to the solar plexus, but I wasn't about to give up that easily. I went back to the ice arena and informed coach Lumley.

He proceeded to march the entire Kent State hockey team into the professor's narrow office. We were crammed into that sardine can so tightly we could hardly breathe. Sitting behind his desk, the professor just stared at us with his mouth wide open.

Once again, I politely asked if we could broadcast the games on the campus radio station. I'm not sure whether the professor was intimidated, or he suddenly realized just how dedicated or crazy I was.

He looked at me very seriously, then smiled and said, "Okay, we'll do it."

That gentleman's name was John Weiser, and I thank Dr. Weiser from the bottom of my heart for his change of heart. It may not have been his cup of tea, but I think he understood what the program meant to me and some other future broadcasters. That one decision by him changed our lives.

Because we were not yet sanctioned by the university as a varsity team, we had to begin as a club sport. Therefore, we were barred from using the Kent State teams' name, the Golden Flashes.

We launched a contest to name the Kent State hockey club. We received many terrific entries, ultimately deciding on the Clippers. It had absolutely nothing to do with Kent State, but it sounded good—the Kent State Clippers.

So now we had an arena, a coach, a team, a radio station, and a name, all within a matter of weeks. While Don conducted practices, drew up the schedule, and made travel arrangements, I, as team president, did the publicity, promotions, public relations, game programs, advertisements, and, most important to me of course, the play-by-play.

I may have been the ignition for Kent State hockey, but Don was the engine, and after we got it off the ground, I had the help of some outstanding fellow students who shared the same fervor I had to make it a success. Don's wife, Elaine, also lent her enthusiastic support. Thanks to everyone's help, I was able to concentrate on the broadcasts.

I finally had the opportunity to hone my skills behind the microphone. We arranged to air all the home games and some road games on WKSU radio. I even convinced the campus television station, WKSU-TV, to broadcast a few games.

My vision for what we called Hockey Night in Kent (borrowed from the hugely popular *Hockey Night in Canada* TV series) was to be different from the mainstream sports on campus, like football, basketball, baseball, and wrestling. I wanted to make the ice arena the coolest place on campus, figuratively speaking.

We put in a lot of hard work, but it was a labor of love. We aimed to run our operation like a professional sports franchise and make the games as entertaining as possible for the fans. Our objective was for every home game to be like a big party, a main event on campus. We played upbeat music before and during games. One of my roommates, Carl, had a phenomenal record collection with hit songs and top groups of that era. We played them on the arena sound system, creating a festive atmosphere.

When fans entered the arena, I wanted them to hear the beat and see the players in their Kent State blue and gold flying down the ice in pregame warmups. Between periods, we had fan contests on the ice with fast food prizes. Once, I hired an organist from the Kent State music department to play during games, just like in the pros. If you closed your eyes, it felt like you were at Madison Square Garden or the Montreal Forum. Another time, I got a pep band to crank up the crowd.

Interestingly, the music soundtrack of our team in the ice arena morphed from pop to heavy metal. The players and the fans loved it. Personally, I was more into The Grass Roots than Led Zeppelin, but on game nights, the place rocked. Why mess with success? It was the early '70s. Long hair was the style, and the Clippers fit the image. The atmosphere at our games was unlike any other sports venue at Kent State. Hockey Night in Kent was a hit.

The players were swept up in it too. They understood the dream I had, and they embraced it. We got the word out about the fun and excitement of Kent State hockey. The student body support exceeded my expectations. I may not have had the stuff to be a hockey player, but I was a hockey play-by-play announcer and, by dint of my being team President, was a hockey entrepreneur and promoter.

That first team that Don assembled was more than competitive and finished the season with a 14-7 record. We had come a long way from that initial tryout. The players' enthusiasm, commitment and heart combined with a great coach made our opening campaign a memorable one. That said, it was not always smooth sailing for the Clippers and me.

* * *

Everything was set for the Clippers' gala premiere. The ice was ready, the game programs were printed, the food and beverage concessions were A-OK, we were expecting a capacity crowd, and I was primed to go on the air for the first-ever Kent State Clippers hockey game.

There was only one hitch. Our flashy blue and gold jerseys had not arrived. What the heck were we supposed to do without team jerseys? We didn't want to look like a bunch of misfits and ragamuffins. With only a few hours before the first puck was to drop, we had just about lost hope for a solution when the coach had a brainstorm. He asked the Kent State football team if we could borrow their practice jerseys, to which, thankfully, they said yes. It wasn't the ideal way to make our debut on campus, but it could have been a lot worse.

In game one, the Clippers were routed 12-3 by the Cleveland Hockey Club. I chalked it up to opening night jitters. Twenty-four hours later, the real Clippers showed up as they bounced back with a resounding 12-2 win over the Parma Hockey Club. We lit the red lamp so often that the fans were going bonkers, erupting with jubilation every time the puck went into the net. Meanwhile, up in the broadcast booth, I was breaking records for the most times a play-by-play announcer exclaimed "He shoots, he scores!" On one call, I think I pulled a muscle.

The second game of the season could not have gone better, and the fans rejoiced as they exited the arena. I knew we had won them over and that they'd come back for more. We were off and running or, in this case, skating.

* * *

In our second season, my senior year, we had gotten permission to travel three broadcasters to Athens, Ohio, to call a game between the Kent State Clippers and the Bobcats of Ohio University.

The trip was extra meaningful to me because my older brother Al had been a star goaltender at OU. For the first time, I was going to see his old haunts, the intimate confines of Bird Arena. Al had told me many stories about the rickety old barn that he, his teammates, and the Ohio faithful had come to embrace. The game we were there to call was the Friday night of Mom's Weekend in Athens. The crowd was abuzz, and Bird Arena was packed to the gills. This showdown was significant to Coach Lumley and the players because it was a tough test against a well-established varsity team. We were not expected to win. However, if we could pull off the upset, or at least keep it competitive, it would be a major lift for the young Kent State hockey program.

Starting Kent State Hockey

We went all out for that radio broadcast. I was to do the play-by-play. My booth mate was Mike Fornes, featured earlier in the book, and we were accompanied by another fellow student named Barry Zuckerman, who went by the name of Big Ken Hamilton on the air. Off the air, we called him Zuck.

We may have been a little ahead of our time when we hooked up Zuck with a wireless microphone, pretty much unheard of in those days. We decided that Zuck would roam the stands, talking to fans and leaning over the boards to interview players during the game. We were excited about our new toy, which we had secured from the audio-visual department at school. And it actually worked!

All was going smoothly up in the booth. Down on the ice was another story. The Clippers were overmatched. They played their hearts out, but they just weren't in the same league as the more experienced Bobcats. It was a 12-5 blowout loss.

We felt bad for Don and the players, but as far as the broadcast was concerned, all three of us were upbeat. We felt it couldn't have gone better. When Mike and I laid down our headsets, we just looked at each other with huge, satisfied grins. We were proud of ourselves. Then we looked down at Zuck in the stands, and we did a group double thumbs-up. We couldn't wait to get back to campus to add highlights of this broadcast to our audition tapes.

Right after we signed off, I called the board engineer at WKSU, a fellow broadcasting student named Dudley. I said gleefully, "Dudley, how did it sound?" Dudley said, "How did *what* sound?" I thought he was kidding around with me. He said he was serious. At the station, they never heard anything. I was dazed like a fighter hit by a punch he never saw coming.

Somehow, some way, something went awry with our telephone, the lifeline of our broadcast. It must have happened just before I started the broadcast, and because there was no other phone in the booth in this time long before cell phones, Dudley couldn't reach us to let us know there was a problem.

A Funny Thing Happened on the Way to the Broadcast Booth

We were sure we had everything covered. We were so vigilant and organized, or so we thought. We had forgotten one crucial item: a backup phone. All that preparation, all that effort. Three hours on the radio, pouring our souls out. Not one word made the airwaves, and there was no recording of it.

After the game, we sat on the stoop of a school building, in stunned disbelief, our heads buried in our hands. There is a silver lining, however, to this story for the hockey club. In the second meeting, the Clippers came within a hair of beating the mighty Bobcats, losing by one goal, 5-4. They say that there are no moral victories in sports, but this game showed the resilience of a brash young team that had no quit.

* * *

I had never seen the Kent State ice arena this alive. It was electric. The joint was jumpin' with the biggest crowd in the short history of the Clippers, standing room only. The fans were stomping their feet and cheering their lungs out, yelling "Go Clippers!"

The game hadn't even started. In fact, the opposing team had not yet arrived. It was just the Kent State Hockey Club warming up on one side of the ice, the other side of the red line empty. It was Friday night of Dad's Weekend at Kent State University. The Clippers had scheduled a blockbuster back-to-back extravaganza with the University of Buffalo. The Clippers were playing well, and Buffalo was a big-name school.

That evening, the hockey gods were not smiling on us.

A snowstorm was coming, and the Buffalo hockey team was stuck in the middle of it. The Buffalo coach called Coach Lumley and told him that it was now snowing heavily on the Ohio Turnpike, driving conditions were becoming hazardous, and they'd had to pull the bus over at a rest stop.

While we were of course concerned for their safety, we had a house full of fans who were growing more impatient by the minute.

I was making final preparations for the broadcast when Don came up to the booth and asked if I would go onto the ice and explain the situation to the crowd over the PA system. Public speaking petrified me. In addition, I didn't want to be the bearer of bad news. Don saw the fear in my eyes and said, "Don't worry, I'll do it myself." He made the announcement, and while the fans understood, their groans made it clear that they weren't happy.

We periodically received updates from the Buffalo coach, but it was not looking good. The players knew what was going on, so they stayed on the ice for what seemed like the longest pregame warmup session of all time. They did what they could to keep the sellout crowd entertained, and we kept making announcements to try to keep the fans in their seats, but they were growing restless.

Then, a light went on in my head. My roommate was an aspiring comedian named Bob Circosta who admired show biz personalities like Johnny Carson, Sammy Davis Jr., and Bob Hope. He was always coming up with material, often waking me up in the middle of the night to tell me a new joke. Other nights, I would hear him practicing his tap dancing in the bathroom because the taps made a neat sound on the tiles. He wanted to be an all-around, all-purpose entertainer.

I hurried out of the broadcast booth and down into Coach Lumley's office in the locker room. I grabbed the telephone and called my roommate.

When he answered, I said, "Bob, you have to do me a big favor."

"What?"

"Come over to the ice arena and perform a comedy routine. You'll have an SRO audience of over fifteen hundred people." The ice arena was right across the street from our apartment at College Towers.

"What in the world are you talking about?"

I told him about the situation and said, "I need you to come over here to entertain the crowd. You'll be like Bob Hope. You'll be a smash hit." I was so desperate at that point I was prepared to tell him anything to get his butt over to the arena. "Bob, I'll do anything for you if you please come over here to the ice arena and put on a show."

He replied, "Steve, I don't have a routine or anything. It's not polished. I wouldn't know what to say."

"You're a pro," I said, "I know you'll come up with something. Please, I need you to get over here as soon as possible."

Reluctantly, he said, "Okay, I'll think of something, and I'll be right over."

When Bob arrived, looking sharp in a sports jacket, I had the PA announcer introduce him: "And now, all the way from across the street, ladies and gentlemen, for your entertainment pleasure while we wait for the University of Buffalo hockey team to arrive, the comedy stylings of Mr. Bob Circosta."

There was a smattering of applause from the crowd. We rolled out a carpet so he wouldn't slip on the ice, and Bob walked out and proceeded to tell some jokes. The fans were not amused. Maybe we shouldn't have put out the carpet so he would have tumbled onto the ice. The crowd would have loved that, but I couldn't do that to my roomie. As Bob's frustration grew, he called the fans a bunch of hockey pucks, imitating the legendary insult comic Don Rickles. The fans booed and began to heckle Bob, stomping their feet in unison.

Poor Bob just walked off and handed the mic to Coach Lumley, who then announced that the game had to be postponed. I was shattered as the huge crowd filed out, but not as shattered as Bob Circosta was. It wasn't his fault. I had put him in an impossible situation, and I felt awful. I think I set his budding comedy career back ten years.

Eventually, he forgave me, and we resumed our friendship. As the years passed, Bob was able to shake off the memory of that night as he went on to become a major success and a face familiar to millions of people as the original host of the hugely popular Home Shopping Network. It couldn't have happened to a nicer guy. I just hope he doesn't break out in hives every time he sees a hockey game.

Starting Kent State Hockey

By the way, Bob, ever the comedian, told me that when he tells his version of the ice arena story, he gets a standing ovation.

* * *

When I announced Kent State hockey, representatives from the opposing teams would provide me with a roster of players' names and numbers. That way, I could identify them on the ice. At times, usually due to a late addition to the team, or just plain laziness, they would not include names next to numbers.

There is an unwritten play-by-play rule that you cannot just call out players' numbers. So, I had to improvise. Instead of pulling names out of thin air, I used names of pals from my old neighborhood in Brooklyn. Here's an example:

> Jacobs skates down the ice. He sends a cross-ice pass to Krongold who races into the Clippers' zone. Krongold with a drop pass to Shonkoff who centers the puck for Ganis. He shoots, he scores!

No one caught on to my shenanigans. As Oliver Hardy would often say to Stan Laurel, "They'll be none the wiser."

* * *

Some years later, when I was a young sportscaster in New York, I received a phone call from Don Lumley. He said, "Are you sitting down? We are now a full-fledged varsity team." Kent State hockey had finally been sanctioned by the university. I was speechless.

As I'm writing this, more than fifty years after the team was founded, Kent State hockey is still going strong. While they have returned to club status, they are now a member of the American Collegiate Hockey Association, and represent the University as the Golden Flashes.

A Funny Thing Happened on the Way to the Broadcast Booth

I'm so proud of what we started back in 1970. I'm even prouder that five students who announced Kent State hockey went on to do play-by-play in the professional ranks. Four in the National Hockey League: Mike Fornes, with the Washington Capitals, the Hartford Whalers, and the Dallas Stars; Rick Peckham, with the Tampa Bay Lightning and the Hartford Whalers; Paul Steigerwald, with the Pittsburgh Penguins; and yours truly, with the New York Islanders. The fifth student, Greg Hallaman, announced in the Central Hockey League, with the Indianapolis Checkers and the Wichita Wind. It shows what you can do with a little initiative, perseverance, and hard work.

* * *

In 2018, I returned to Kent State for a hockey team reunion. It was my first time back on campus since I graduated in 1972. Chalk that up to a busy career in sportscasting. Many of the original team members showed up. Seeing them brought back fond memories and I was so glad I made the trip. One of the players even presented me with an original team jersey that he had worn on game nights. I was touched by the gesture.

The only disappointment was learning that the play-by-play portion of the game broadcasts had stopped. The game video was available but without announcers calling the action. I was inspired to make a donation to help resurrect the announcing of the games so that students would have the same opportunity I and others had to get hands-on experience doing hockey play-by-play. I also got to mentor some of the student-broadcasters, providing them with tips on improving their on-air skills.

It took my retirement to finally make it back to KSU. The trip was long overdue.

* * *

I dedicate this chapter to Coach Don Lumley, to the memory of the team's biggest booster, Don's beloved wife Elaine Lumley, and to every original member of the Kent State hockey club. Thanks for helping a kid from Brooklyn realize his dream.

A Funny Thing Happened on the Way to the Broadcast Booth

What Do I Do?

In 1972, an attorney named Nick Mileti, who already owned the Cleveland Cavaliers, the Cleveland Barons, the Cleveland Arena, and WWWE radio, acquired a franchise in a newly-formed major league known as the World Hockey Association.

The WHA was a rebel force that had the brass to go head-to-head with the long-established National Hockey League by raiding the NHL of their biggest names, like Gordie Howe and Bobby Hull. Mileti called his team the Crusaders and signed NHL star Gerry Cheevers. Crusader games were to be broadcast on Mileti's radio station, a 50,000-watt Class A clear channel powerhouse that could be heard in thirty-eight states and Canada.

The moment the Crusaders came into existence, I was determined to become their play-by-play announcer and fulfil my goal of calling professional hockey. They were my number one target.

A Funny Thing Happened on the Way to the Broadcast Booth

Cleveland was my second home. I was very familiar with the territory and I had many friends in Northeast Ohio. How fabulous it would be to announce in the same city and on the same radio station as my early mentor, Joe Tait, the voice of the Cavaliers. I was freshly graduated from Kent State, only a forty-five-minute drive from downtown Cleveland, and I had already broadcast from the Cleveland Arena booth when I called a couple of Springfield Kings-Cleveland Barons minor league games. I really had my heart set on getting this job.

Following graduation, I had returned home to Brooklyn, and immediately mailed an audition tape to the Crusaders. I also sent tapes and resumés to various minor league hockey teams throughout the country. I found out the hard way that you had to be extremely patient. I waited as calmly as I could for a response. I waited and waited and waited. Nothing. Not one nibble.

Every day, I would run to the mailbox and every day I was disappointed. It was a long, hot summer. Then, just as I was about to give up all hope for that hockey season, there was a tug on the line.

The Greensboro Generals of the Eastern Hockey League liked what they had heard on my tape and they flew me down to North Carolina for a face-to-face interview. The Generals operated under the same ownership as the Carolina Cougars of the ABA and shared the Greensboro Coliseum. The president of the two clubs was Carl Scheer, who later worked as President and General Manager of both the Denver Nuggets and the Charlotte Hornets, and would go on to become one of the most admired executives in the NBA.

Carl and I had a terrific conversation in his office at the coliseum, and he subsequently informed me that the job was mine. I was on top of the world. After all that agita, just like that, I was a professional hockey play-by-play man. It was too good to be true.

Cleveland was still lurking in the back of my mind, but I couldn't pass up this opportunity.

I bid farewell to Brooklyn, moved down to Greensboro, found myself a nice place to live, and began preparations to announce for

What Do I Do?

the Generals. The team welcomed me with open arms, and Carl even lent me his car. Before I got my apartment, he had invited me to stay at his home with his wife and family. It was Southern hospitality at its finest.

Once at a restaurant in Greensboro, I ran into the spectacular Billy Cunningham, who was then playing for the Carolina Cougars. Billy was a legend down in Tar Heel country, having starred for the University of North Carolina. He had bolted from the NBA for the ABA, causing quite a splash. Carolinians were wearing "Billy C Is Back" buttons.

Billy and I started talking, and I told him I had just been hired to do the Generals games on the radio. I also told him I was from Brooklyn. His eyes widened and he smiled broadly. Billy was also a native son. In fact, he was one of Brooklyn's hometown heroes, out of Erasmus Hall High School.

He said, "Steve, take these," flipping me the keys to his glittering new sports car. "Take it for a spin," he said.

I replied, "Billy, I can't. What if I wreck it?"

"Don't worry, you won't wreck it."

As tempting as the offer was, I just couldn't do it. I thanked Billy for his kindness, and as I said goodbye, I thought, "Is this really happening? Can people be this friendly?" It was such a delight to be in Greensboro to begin my career.

One night, I attended a preseason basketball game in nearby Charlotte. The Generals set me up with a pass in the broadcast booth as the Carolina Cougars were playing the NBA's Atlanta Hawks. Julius Erving, a rookie straight out of the University of Massachusetts, was playing for Atlanta. Not many people remember that Dr. J played for the Hawks just before he signed with the New York Nets of the ABA. What are the odds that four years later, I would be announcing for the Nets when Dr. J won the ABA's final championship?

Also that night, the voice of the Cougars, Bob Lamey, who would later become the longtime radio play-by-play announcer for the

Indianapolis Colts, tried to convince me to get involved in a fake feud with him to drum up publicity. I thought about it for a minute, then said, "Bob, it's just not me." He laughed and said, "No problem, Steve, I understand." I got a kick out of him asking me, though.

I hadn't been in Greensboro very long, and the hockey season hadn't even started, but I already sensed a warmth about this town. I came to love Greensboro and the down-home feeling I got from being there.

Then it happened.

* * *

As badly as I wanted that Cleveland Crusaders job, I had pretty much given up on them. By the end of the summer, they still had not contacted me.

I learned a valuable lesson as my career developed: You can't take it personally. When applying for an announcing job, you have to realize that certain matters are not immediate priorities for teams. They have endless issues to tackle, particularly a brand-new franchise. The broadcasts, as important as they are, might be the last item they address. Being naive about all of this at the time, I simply assumed they weren't interested in my services. Well, that was not the case.

The Crusaders had begun to seek a play-by-play announcer just a matter of days before their opening game. After waiting all summer, I had decided to pounce on the opportunity offered by the Greensboro Generals, thinking another one might never come. There were so few broadcasting jobs, I honestly believed that most if not all young play-by-play announcers in my shoes would have done the same thing. Well, wouldn't you know it? The Crusaders called.

Team official Bob Brown, Nick Mileti's chief lieutenant, wanted to know if I could come to Cleveland to audition for the job.

I was very conflicted on what to do. I had a job with the Greensboro Generals and the team had been so welcoming. The

What Do I Do?

Cleveland position, however, was my dream job. I agonized over the situation. After thinking it over, I decided to proceed with the audition. I figured I could decide later which direction to go if I got the Crusaders job.

I flew to Cleveland for the tryout. Instead of just relying on my submitted audition tape, the Crusaders wanted to hear me call a live game. On opening night, the Cavaliers' play-by-play man, Joe Tait, announced the Crusaders game live on the radio at one end of the Cleveland Arena while I made an audition tape of the game at the opposite end.

Built in 1937, the Cleveland Arena had been home to the Cleveland Barons of the American Hockey League for decades. Despite its antiquated appearance, it oozed character and personality. The fans' close proximity to the ice, the chicken wire railing above the boards, as opposed to the customary plexiglass, the mellifluous tones of the organ music, and the smell of hot dogs, all merged to create a decidedly intimate atmosphere. (By the way, the hot dogs were amazing.) It was a throwback to classic old-time hockey, and it was like stepping back in time.

The arena stood at 3717 Euclid Avenue in a gritty area of downtown Cleveland. The official seating capacity for hockey was ninety-three hundred, but sometimes they managed to cram in a few hundred more. The broadcast booths were located in the end zones, instead of the sides, which was unusual for hockey. The announcers looked down at the back of a goaltender. It was a challenge to call games there because players on offense were skating towards you, and you couldn't see their jersey numbers. Despite that, I really loved the place. Besides, back then, helmets were not mandatory, so I could recognize players' faces and hair.

What I really liked were the Crusaders' unique uniforms. The jerseys were purple, black, and white and featured a knight on a horse.

It was difficult not to be swept up in the euphoria of opening night. To a young hockey announcer like myself, it was exhilarating.

A Funny Thing Happened on the Way to the Broadcast Booth

Sitting in my two-by-four broadcast booth, I was soaking it all in and looking out over the sellout crowd. The anticipation was building, and when the Crusaders came bursting onto the ice, the noise level was deafening. Cleveland was no longer a minor league hockey town and the Cleveland faithful were showing their appreciation.

As the inaugural puck was dropped, I turned on my tape recorder and off I went into hockey heaven. I was never more psyched in my life to call a game.

When the Crusaders scored their first goal, the crowd went wild. I looked down and saw people hugging each other. The old arena on Euclid was literally vibrating. Big-time hockey had finally arrived, and I was hooked. My longing to announce in Cleveland grew stronger. I knew this was something special and I wanted to be a part of it.

The Crusaders were triumphant with a dazzling 2-0 shutout over the Quebec Nordiques. The fans went home happy, and I handed my audition tape to Bob Brown.

It had been an emotional day, and I was wired up when I got to the hotel, Jim Swingo's Keg and Quarter. I've never forgotten that name.

Getting to sleep wasn't easy, and early the next morning I was abruptly awakened by the loud ring of the phone. In a gravelly voice, I answered, "Hello?" It was a representative from the Crusaders, who asked me to come to their headquarters in the Cleveland Arena. When I arrived, I was escorted to a large private office that was dimly lit. Thanks to some streaks of sunlight dancing through the window, I could make out a big desk at the other end.

Suddenly, a high-backed leather chair swiveled around, and sitting in it was Nick Mileti, the Crusaders' owner. He was a powerful and influential businessman and the number one sports entrepreneur in Cleveland.

Mileti got right to the point. "Okay," he said. "I'll give you $9,500 for the first year, $11,000 for the second year, and $12,000 for the

What Do I Do?

third year." My heart was pounding so hard, I thought it was going to burst through my chest. This was what I had worked for since I first fell in love with sportscasting as a child, when practicing play-by-play with my brothers.

The problem was I had already accepted the Greensboro job and was set to announce the season opener in a couple of weeks. I didn't think the Crusaders would act so fast. There was no, "Why not take a day or two to think it over?" Their season was underway, and they needed to fill the position pronto.

I had to make a quick decision. Even though I had a great job in Greensboro, I couldn't pass up this opportunity. I was concerned about how to handle this conundrum, but I decided to go with what was always my first choice, the Crusaders.

Later that day I flew back to Greensboro and dealt with the situation as openly and honestly as I could. I was dreading the conversation, but I sat down with Carl Scheer in his office and explained everything that had happened.

After I poured out my guts, instead of being angry, Carl just looked at me and smiled.

He said, "Steve, you're not going to believe this, but the same exact thing happened to me when I was just starting out. I was faced with a similar dilemma, and I had to make a decision. I put everything else aside and made the choice based on what would be best for me. I completely understand where you're coming from. Go with our blessings. No hard feelings. I would have done the same thing you did."

I can't thank Carl Scheer enough for his graciousness. I had a short but memorable experience in Greensboro. Carl made my transition to Cleveland far less awkward than I thought it would be. I am forever grateful to him.

It was off to Cleveland to start my broadcasting journey, where more adventures and misadventures were on the horizon.

A Funny Thing Happened on the Way to the Broadcast Booth

Breaking the Ice

My goal was to broadcast professional hockey after graduating from college. I was thrilled to launch my career announcing for the Cleveland Crusaders in the friendly confines of the Cleveland Arena.

My on-air debut was the Crusaders' second game as a WHA franchise. Since Joe Tait had announced the first game in Crusader history, he opened the radio broadcast to pass the baton and introduce me as the voice of the Crusaders. It was only fitting, since he was the one who gave me my first big break while I was still in college. Joe had been a graduate assistant at Ohio University before turning pro. There, he befriended my older brother Al, a radio and TV major, who was a goaltender/play-by-play announcer for the school's hockey team.

A Funny Thing Happened on the Way to the Broadcast Booth

As the Crusaders skated onto the ice for pregame warmups, Joe and I squeezed into the tight broadcast booth overlooking the end zone. My heart raced as I counted down the seconds to the beginning of my career. I knew I would remember this moment for the rest of my life. I tried to take deep breaths to settle my nerves. The radio engineer looked at Joe and then raised his hand. With his fingers, he counted—five, four, three, two, one, then pointed at Joe, the universal signal for "You're on the air." There was no turning back now.

Joe's first words came out of his mouth in an uncharacteristically disjointed fashion. He said, "Good evvv-ning eee-vree-body," instead of his usual polished "Good evening, everybody." It caught me by surprise. I was supposed to be the nervous Nellie in the booth, not Joe Tait.

Joe laughed, shrugged it off, and proceeded to give me a warm and poignant welcome to the Cleveland sports scene. His exact words were, "In the old days down at Ohio University, when you needed an Albert to call some hockey, you had to go get Al Albert out of the goal. Here, it's much easier. You simply turn to your left, and say, 'Steve Albert, it's all yours.'"

Joe had such a command of the language and a wonderful way with words. His introduction was perfect, and it was heartwarming. When Joe made his on-air gaffe with his first words, I must tell you, it immediately put me at ease. My heart rate plummeted to normal. I felt like myself again, and I was able to take the reins from Joe and start broadcasting Cleveland Crusaders hockey with confidence and composure.

I was always curious about that moment before my debut with the Crusaders. Joe was the consummate pro and rarely made mistakes on the air, particularly right at the beginning of a broadcast. That's when an announcer is really on his or her toes, acutely focused on getting the broadcast off on the right foot. There's an old broadcasting adage: Start the show clean and end the show clean.

As the years went by, I would occasionally ask him if he did it on purpose. Joe would just smile and zip his lips with his hands. To this day, I firmly believe that Joe intentionally muffed the start of the broadcast. I think he did it to take the pressure off me.

Thanks to Joe Tait, I couldn't have had a better debut. He assisted countless other young broadcasting hopefuls. Sadly, we lost Joe in 2021. He truly was one of the greats, on and off the air.

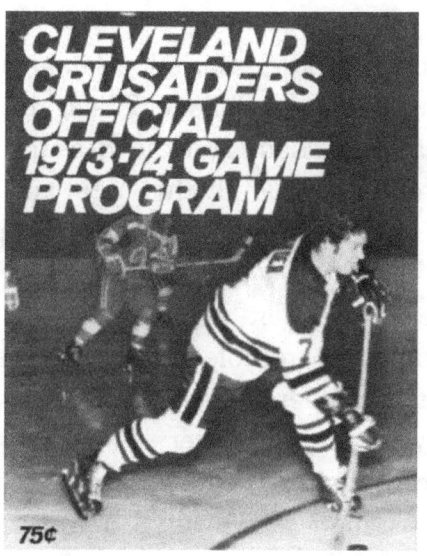

I still have a Crusaders game program as a warm reminder of my early years in broadcasting.

With Joe's boost, my career was off and running, in a renegade league that lasted until 1979. I was there for the Crusader's first three seasons. In 1975, I returned home to become the television voice of the ABA's New York Nets. The Crusaders remained in Cleveland until 1976 and then relocated to Minnesota, where they dissolved a year later.

And what became of the Greensboro Generals? After my first season with the Crusaders, the Generals and three other teams bolted the Eastern League and formed the Southern Hockey League.

A Funny Thing Happened on the Way to the Broadcast Booth

The team struggled with financial problems and moved to a smaller arena where they languished in last place. The Generals and the Southern Hockey League went out of business in 1977.

In sports, teams come and go and leagues come and go. Their impact on so many people, including announcers, however, is everlasting.

* * *

During the World Hockey Association's inaugural season in 1972, the Crusaders had a game in Philadelphia against the Blazers, who were originally based in Miami and known as the Screaming Eagles. It was the home opener for Philly that night and there was a pretty sizable crowd on hand. I was up in my broadcast perch and ready to call the action.

On paper, the Blazers were an impressive team. They had gone out and gotten some recognizable names from the NHL, like former Boston Bruin Derek Sanderson, goaltender Bernie Parent from the Philadelphia Flyers, and another ex-Bruin, John "Pie Face" McKenzie. Sanderson had signed a five-year, $2.6 million contract, at the time the most money ever paid to a professional athlete.

On this first night, the Zamboni got to the arena late and made ice that could not support the weight of the players. The ice actually cracked open. Despite the pedigrees of their players, the Blazers could not play ice hockey without ice.

I never found out why the Zamboni was late—did it miss the bus or oversleep? The game was rescheduled for the next night. I signed off by saying we would be back on the air with the game the following night.

The following night arrived and, thankfully, so did the Zamboni, and it was on time. To prove to the fans that the ice was suitable for professional hockey, the Blazers trotted out a guy dressed as what was commonly known at the time as an Eskimo. Whether he was truly Inuit or an office intern who put on this costume, I do not know.

He was carrying a rather formidable harpoon, which he proceeded to ram into the ice to prove that it was good to go. Does anyone wonder why this franchise folded after one season?

* * *

You may find this difficult to believe, but in the Crusaders' third season, another ice-related incident occurred, only this time on Cleveland's home ice.

Team owner Nick Mileti had built the $36 million Richfield Coliseum in Richfield, Ohio, located between Cleveland and Akron. It was a beautiful structure that was christened during a black-tie concert event featuring Frank Sinatra that I was lucky to attend. I remember thinking, "So, this is how the big time feels."

The Coliseum, new home to the Crusaders and the Cavaliers, had a capacity of 18,544 for hockey, a far cry from the ninety-three hundred-seat Cleveland Arena. The only problem? It was miles away from everything and there wasn't a lot around it, like restaurants or hotels.

The Crusaders were ready for their opening night in their luxurious new digs. It was the home opener for the '74–'75 season, and I was primed and ready for action up in the broadcast booth. From my standpoint, the best thing about the new building was that the announcers' booths were not in the end zones, as they were at the old arena downtown. They were high above the surface but near center ice. In addition, they weren't really booths per se, but tables out in the open. It was a good way to get to know the fans.

Before the game, the teams warmed up as usual, but we were informed that the players were a little uneasy because the ice was too soft. I could see from my new broadcast position that patches of the ice looked watery and discolored. The opening face-off was delayed while maintenance workers scrambled to rectify the problem. I had already started the broadcast. In those days, once we began, it was all me. We didn't throw it back to the studio because there was no one there to throw it to. Knowing that there was a hockey broadcast that night, all the announcers and DJs went home. Oh, and did I mention that I was flying solo? That's right, for the three years I was there, except for one or two games, I worked alone.

I figured I would have to tap dance on the air for a few minutes while they repaired the ice. I was okay with that, but three hours later, I was still trying to fill the airwaves.

To kill time while I kept the broadcast going, I interviewed what must have been every fan, vendor, and usher in the coliseum that night. That may have been the longest delay "stretch" in broadcasting history.

Finally, it was announced that the game was postponed and rescheduled for the following night. At least you couldn't blame this one on the Zamboni—it was right on time.

* * *

One night at the Richfield Coliseum, the Cleveland Crusaders were going against the aptly named Minnesota Fighting Saints, and a fight broke out on the ice. What a shocker.

It was my job to describe it on the radio. Within seconds, another fight broke out. Then, another, and another—four fights going on at the same time. As players hammered away at each other, the Minnesota coach climbed over the glass behind the bench, did a swan dive into the crowd, and started whaling away at the fans. So now we had five fights going on simultaneously. I then heard a commotion to my right, where the visiting broadcast table was located, and saw the Minnesota announcers, including 1960 U.S. Olympic gold medalist Jack McCartan, in a brouhaha with the Crusaders faithful. That made six fights. Somehow, I managed to continue calling all this mayhem.

Later in life, I jokingly told people that's how I got the job calling fights on Showtime. I'd say, "They called to ask if I would be interested in being their boxing announcer. Naturally, my first question was, 'How many fights do I have to call at the same time?' They said, 'Just one, of course.' I said, 'Really, just one? Piece of cake, where do I sign?'"

That may have been a bit of a tale, but calling so many fights in the WHA prepared me well for my future endeavor.

* * *

We had finally made it back home after an extraordinarily long and exhausting road trip with the Crusaders. It was one of those punishing four- or five-city journeys through the United States and Canada that felt like it would never end. There was no rest for the weary, as the Crusaders were to go right back on the ice the very next night at the Cleveland Arena. The team was dog tired and so was its radio play-by-play announcer. But, as they say in the business, "The show must go on." Trooper that I am, I made it through the opening period. What happened just after that was cause for concern.

Here's how it went down. I said, "So that's the end of the first period with the score, Cleveland two and . . ." I drew a complete blank. For the life of me, I could not remember who the Crusaders were playing. As my brain freeze persisted, I thought, "I'll just look at the scoreboard. It'll say the opponent's name on it." The scoreboard read "Home" and "Visitors." I started to have an anxiety attack. Then it occurred to me, there are always a few stragglers skating around on the ice before going to the locker room—I'll look for the visiting jerseys. There was not a soul out there. My mind was in such disarray that I never thought to look down at the rosters on the table in front of me.

Running out of options, I looked over to my statistician, "Steady" Eddie Jelenich, to rescue me from my play-by-play predicament. He was doubled over on the floor, laughing. Finally, I went to my last recourse.

I said, "Folks, we just returned from a really long road trip. We were in a lot of different cities. I'll be honest. I cannot remember who the Crusaders are playing." Just as I said it—bam!—I remembered. The Chicago Cougars.

It was the most embarrassing moment of my career. To make matters worse, the disc jockeys at the station thought they'd have a little fun with it, so they kept playing the sequence over and over again on WWWE radio the next day. That night, I learned something that stayed with me for the rest of my career. If you're in broadcasting, you'd better be able to laugh at yourself.

Tall Stories

I was a well-travelled play-by-play man—and that was just with the Nets. There were stops in Uniondale, New York, Piscataway, New Jersey, and East Rutherford, New Jersey. Players, coaches and general managers frequently came and went, but there were two constants: trainer Fritz Massman and the television announcers. For a majority of my thirteen years behind the team's mic, my TV broadcast partner was Bill Raftery.

The man affectionately called Raf broke into the business after a colorful career as head basketball coach at Seton Hall University. As an announcer, he was astute but also gregarious and funny. You could just tell that he loved what he did for a living.

Raf was a stellar all-around athlete who had starred in basketball, soccer, and baseball at Saint Cecilia High School in Kearny, New Jersey. Quite the schoolboy legend, Raf was. He was all-state in three sports and became the all-time leading basketball scorer in state history, holding that distinction for thirty-five years before the record was finally broken.

Opening up a New Jersey Nets telecast with the personable Bill Raftery (left) on WOR-TV (Channel 9).

His all-around athleticism included golf, but our busy schedule made it tough to play during the season. One time, however, we were in Los Angeles and had a rare day off before the Nets played the Lakers. Raf asked me to join him for eighteen holes at one of LA's prestigious golf links.

I reluctantly said okay, with the disclaimer "But Raf, I'm not really very good."

"Don't worry about it. We'll have fun."

We arrived at the golf course on a breathtaking morning in Southern California. The sun was shining and the sky was a deep blue. It was heavenly, especially after coming from the cold, gray, wintry East Coast.

As we were approaching the first tee, I broke out my trusty tube of Bain de Soleil suntan gel. I was as pale as a ghost, and I wasn't going to let an opportunity like this pass me by. While Raf was preparing to tee off, I was off to the side behind him, coating my hands with the gooey substance and greasing up my face. Raf teed off with a solid drive down the middle. It was my turn. I stepped up to where Raf had just stood and planted my ball down carefully on the tee. (I was tempted to "address the ball" by saying "Hellooo, ball," like Ed Norton did in a famous *Honeymooners* episode, but decided otherwise.) I went into my backswing, and as I followed through, my driver went soaring out of my hands about fifty yards straight down the fairway. The ball, of course, never moved an inch.

I had apparently applied so much of the greasy gel to my face that my hands became slicker than an oil field. I hadn't taken the time to wipe them off for fear of holding up the anxious-looking foursome waiting behind us. I don't think I ever saw Raf laugh as hard as when that club went flying through my fingers and sailed through the air. Not only that, but the four total strangers behind us were convulsing. I wanted to crawl into a sand trap and bury myself. Raf never let me forget it.

* * *

Rich Kelley was a seven-foot center who briefly wore a Nets uniform when they played at the ninety-five hundred-seat Rutgers Athletic Center in Piscataway, New Jersey. Kelley was a number seven overall pick by the New Orleans Jazz out of Stanford who played eleven years in the NBA. His best year was as a rookie with the Jazz, when he averaged 15.7 points and 12.8 rebounds, good for second in the league on the boards that year.

Kelley's cameo in the Garden State was not the finest year for the Nets, who finished dead last in the Atlantic Division.

Despite that, the seven-footer had become a popular personality, and the Nets marketing team came up with the idea of handing out life-size posters of Kelley as a giveaway to fans.

You may not believe this, but on the day of Rich Kelley Poster Night . . . Rich Kelley was traded to the Phoenix Suns. The Nets were stuck with ten thousand life-size seven-foot posters. To rub salt in the wound, the following season Kelley helped the Suns to the Pacific Division title. I've heard of a player being posterized, but an entire team?

* * *

Eddie Johnson, aka EJ, is a good golfer, although I never hit the links with him. I took him at his word. I do know from first-hand knowledge that he was a deadly sharpshooter on the basketball court, having announced many of his games when he played in the NBA. I also know that he was a terrific broadcast partner.

EJ is a native Chicagoan who starred at the University of Illinois and went on to play 17 years in the NBA. He scored the second most career points (19,202) for players who never participated in the NBA All-Star Game and he was the league's Sixth Man of the Year in 1989 as a player for the Phoenix Suns.

Eddie appeared to have a photographic memory. While I had to rely on reams of notes and anecdotes at the broadcast table, when I looked over to EJ, it was just him and an empty table. It was all stored away in his head. I always marveled at that. He had an innate ability to break down players' strengths and weaknesses. His knowledge of the game was *nonpareil*.

When I came on board as the Suns TV play-by-play announcer, the team was floundering. They had gone five straight years without making the playoffs. It was five more years by the time I retired. Despite those hard times, I don't think I ever had more fun calling NBA games. Eddie Johnson had a lot to do with that.

Tall Stories

I typically played it straight when calling the action. At times, I couldn't resist going for the funny bone, sometimes catching EJ "off guard," if you'll pardon the basketball pun.

Nothing was planned or rehearsed. It came organically. For example, during a broadcast, producer Bob Adlhoch played a recorded piece in which Suns star Devin Booker described how he would spin the ball to find the seams before he shot it. EJ had a basketball at the ready to show how *he* liked to hold the ball when he played. When Eddie finished, I asked him if he could demonstrate how today, as an announcer, he liked to hold the microphone. He looked at me and almost lost it. He did not expect that question.

Then there was the time a Suns player passed the ball to nobody. The ball just sailed into the stands. Without missing a beat, I said that he passed the ball to Claude Rains. The savvy EJ knew exactly what I meant. Claude Rains was the movie star who played the lead character in *The Invisible Man*. In this particular case, Eddie was laughing so hard, he couldn't speak. From that moment on, every time a player threw a pass and no teammate was on the receiving end, EJ referred to it as a pass to Claude Rains.

When games turned grim for the Suns, I occasionally detoured to humor to distract from the score. Eddie did the same. His own wit and sarcasm often had Bob Adlhoch, along with Director Dan Siekmann and producer David Hughes, in stitches. Levity was always what got me through announcing for struggling teams. Unfortunately, I had a lot of experience. When I did TV play-by-play for the New Jersey Nets in rough times, the team's radio voice, Howard David, and I would soothe the loses by trading zingers and one-liners on team buses and planes. My broadcast partners with the New Orleans Hornets, Gil McGregor and Jordy Hultberg, also used humor when appropriate. On or off the air, laughter was the great elixir. EJ is cut from the same cloth.

Announcing with Eddie Johnson was like sitting next to a friend in the stands, conversing about the game and life. He understood that it wasn't only about informing the viewers, but entertaining them as well. Simply put, he got it.

My Phoenix Suns broadcast partner Eddie Johnson (left) is a former NBA Sixth Man of the Year, but he's an all-star announcer and person.

* * *

My first basketball broadcast partner was a true gentleman named Bob Goldsholl. We called the ABA's New York Nets together, then continued our partnership in the Garden State when the Nets moved across the Hudson River in the late 1970s.

Bob had pitched in the minor leagues after leading New York University to the College World Series. Like Bill Raftery and Eddie Johnson, he had made a smooth transition to broadcasting.

One time, Bob and I were invited to a party being thrown by Nets center Mike Gminski and his wife at their home in New Jersey.

G-Man, as he was known, was an amiable guy who would come over to me before every telecast and pat my head for good luck. The way the Nets were playing, I'm not sure it was working.

Bob and I were sitting on a couch at the Gminskis' party. Next to Bob on an end table sat a bowl of snacks, or so it seemed. Bob took a big handful and stuffed it into his mouth. Just then, the seven-foot Gminski walked over to Bob with a big grin.

Gminski asked as he pointed to the bowl, "Bob, do you know what that is?"

Bob said, "What?"

Mike replied, "Potpourri!"

In other words, it was some decorative substance made from wood shavings.

Bob merely said, "It's good."

The guy must have had a cast iron stomach. Man, I could have used that. I might still be working today. I think I single-handedly kept Maalox in business during my career. Had I eaten potpourri, I would have been out for the season.

* * *

There was no way the Nets could fill the void left by Dr. J following the ABA-NBA merger. But they caught lightning in a bottle with the acquisition of Robert "Bubbles" Hawkins, a former fifty-first pick by the Golden State Warriors in the 1975 draft.

Bubbles was cut by the Warriors just before the start of the '76–'77 campaign and couldn't latch on with another team. He was close to seeking another line of work. The Nets, who were struggling mightily in their first NBA season, decided to take a flyer on Mr. Hawkins. What did they have to lose? They were in desperate need of a guard.

On February 7, 1977, I was behind the mic for a 93-89 win over the New Orleans Jazz as Bubbles erupted for a career high forty-four points. I remember the jubilation of calling that game in the midst of a season to forget. He would average 19.3 points and even competed against the legendary "Pistol Pete" Maravich in a televised game of horse at the NBA All-Star game.

Bubbles was an overnight sensation. However, Bubbles's bubble burst, as he played in only fifteen games the following season when the Nets moved from New York to New Jersey. Hawkins was let go after clashing with head coach Kevin Loughery.

Yes, Bubbles Hawkins came and went, seemingly in the blink of an eye. But for a fleeting moment, he brought a ray of hope to a faltering franchise. Not only that, but how many play-by-play announcers got the chance to say Bubbles on the air every night for a whole season?

* * *

Bill Fitch was a two-time NBA coach of the year who guided the Boston Celtics to the 1981 championship. He ranks tenth all-time in victories, but he also ranks second all-time in losses. The latter can partly be attributed to his early years as head coach of the fledgling Cleveland Cavaliers. For example, when he was the Cavs' first coach in the 1970-71 season, the team went 15-67. He came to New Jersey in 1989, and the Nets finished the '89-'90 season with a record of 17-65.

Those were challenging games to call on TV. They were also trying times for Bill Fitch.

One night at the Meadowlands Arena, Bill flew off the handle and hotly disputed a close call with one of the referees and was promptly told to leave the premises. Off he went to the locker room to watch the rest of the game on television, with yours truly describing the action. I was still talking about his outburst on the court, saying that the first thing he would probably do is take a bunch of Rolaids to settle his stomach. After all, as the old TV commercial slogan went, "How do you spell relief? R-O-L-A-I-D-S."

Prior to the next game, I was sitting at the courtside table getting ready to start the broadcast when a hand reached in and dropped off a pack of Rolaids. I looked over, and who do I see with a big smile on his face? That's right, Bill Fitch.

He went on to be named one of the top ten head coaches in NBA history, and in 2019 he reached the mountaintop when he was inducted into the Naismith Basketball Hall of Fame. Bill Fitch, who passed away in 2022 at the age of eighty-nine, was an honorable man who took his job seriously, but not himself.

* * *

I had a soft spot in my heart for the referees in the NBA. There was one in particular who stood out to me.

Dick Bavetta, a former Wall Street broker, found that breaking into the highly-competitive world of NBA officiating wasn't easy. For ten years, he reffed games in the Wall Street League as well as in the public and Catholic high school leagues. He spent an additional nine years refereeing in the old Eastern League.

After being turned down by the NBA for eight consecutive years, going from tryout to tryout, his dream finally came true in 1975. Dick made his NBA debut at Madison Square Garden for a game between the Knicks and the Celtics.

He went on to become one of the most well-respected referees in the league, officiating for thirty-nine years in the NBA. Dick never missed an assigned game and holds the league record for most officiated games with 2,635. He was known as the Cal Ripken Jr. of referees.

As fellow-Brooklynites, Dick and I formed an immediate bond. Whenever he would referee a game I was announcing, he would walk over to me out on the basketball court and hand me a rolled up napkin that contained an assortment of typical old-fashioned Italian cookies. It was a kinship thing. He was like family.

A Funny Thing Happened on the Way to the Broadcast Booth

If there was an all-star mensch team in the NBA, it's a cinch that Dick Bavetta would be the captain.

* * *

When I was the TV announcer for the Golden State Warriors, I was fortunate to call games involving future Hall of Famers Tim Hardaway, Mitch Richmond, and Chris Mullin. I'm sure Warriors radio play-by-play man, Greg Papa, felt the same. The team was coached by another future Hall of Famer, the innovative Don Nelson, who emphasized a fast-paced attack, lots of running, a motion offense, and sharing of the ball.

In the first game I broadcast for the Warriors, they beat the Denver Nuggets, 162-158, in Denver. It was the highest combined score in NBA history for a regulation game. After the telecast, when I finally caught my breath, I asked my color commentator, Jim Barnett, if this was going to happen every night with this team. I said, "I may have to replace you with an oxygen tank."

The trio of Tim, Mitch, and Chris was at the core of this super exciting brand of basketball. They had Bay Area fans in a frenzy, and I was in play-by-play paradise. That threesome was so awe-inspiring that the *San Francisco Examiner* decided to hold a contest to give them a nickname. The entries poured in, to the tune of more than 1,500. The prize was four prime tickets to a Warriors game.

The team asked me to host the selection presentation on the court of the Oakland-Alameda County Coliseum, home of the Warriors, in which Tim, Mitch, and Chris would choose the winner of the contest.

Some of the candidates I offered to the three players were the Ultimate Warriors, Three-Mendous, and the Dunkin' Go-nuts. These were met with eye rolls or blank stares. Then I uttered the words "Run TMC," submitted by Warriors fan Pete Elman. Everything just stopped. The guys looked at each other, then looked at me, saying almost in unison, "Yeah, that could work." I had pretty much the same reaction they had.

Run DMC was a popular hip-hop group at the time, and the name just seemed to fit. The *T* of course was for Tim, *M* for Mitch, and *C* for Chris, and when they played, man, did they run. The nickname caught on like wildfire.

The Warriors of Run TMC did not win a championship, but they were the hottest ticket in town and sold out the arena every night. Even today, the trio of Run TMC—and that dynamic era of Warriors basketball—are still cherished by the fans of the Bay Area.

So many people became Warriors fans because of Run TMC. On top of that, whenever those teams scored 120 points or more, the fans got free pizza. I remember that well, because after the games, I would ask the fans sitting behind the broadcast table for leftovers.

Hosting the nickname contest for the dazzling trio. The winner was "Run TMC," which stood for Tim (Hardaway), Mitch (Richmond) and Chris (Mullin). From left, Mitch Richmond, Tim Hardaway, Chris Mullin and me.

It's hard to believe, but in 1991 the Warriors traded Mitch Richmond to Sacramento. Run TMC was gone but not forgotten.

* * *

Shortly after I arrived in Phoenix in August 2012 to start my new job as the Suns television play-by-play man, I stopped by the team's

A Funny Thing Happened on the Way to the Broadcast Booth

home, then known as the US Airways Center. It must have been a hundred and ten degrees that day. The Suns' legendary Hall of Fame radio announcer, Al McCoy, greeted me with a hug. Al was revered in Phoenix. His resonant voice, descriptive calls, and signature catchphrases like "shazam," "wham, bam, slam," and "heartbreak hotel" captivated fans, making him as popular as some of the greatest all-time Suns players like Charles Barkley, Steve Nash, Walter Davis, and Kevin Johnson. That kind of acclaim is rare.

Al took me under his wing and introduced me to almost every member of the Suns organization. I mean, we went from cubicle to cubicle throughout the entire Suns office complex. And get this, as Al escorted me around, he identified every person by name, which I thought was uncanny. I said to myself, "This guy has a superhuman memory. I have to find out his secret."

When we were finally finished, I turned to Al and said, "Al, this was unbelievable. I am incredibly impressed. When you introduced me to each individual, you knew everyone's name. How could you possibly pull that off?"

He just looked at me and said in his familiar deep tone, "Steve, each desk had a nameplate."

I blamed it on the heat.

That Al went out of his way to introduce me to so many people showed what kind of a person he was. I was fortunate to be around Al McCoy on a regular basis as I closed out my career. Sure, we had exchanged pleasantries through the years when I was announcing for other NBA teams, but broadcasting for the same team was different. I saw what a positive impact he had on the community and how truly loved he was by the Phoenix fans. I also saw what a caring, close-knit family he had, and I appreciated their kindness toward me.

After my stint with the Suns, I retired and went home to New York. I missed hanging out with Al, particularly at my favorite Phoenix delicatessen, Chompie's. (I also missed the deli, so much so that I named my dog Chompie in honor of the place.) Al and I talked about everything over our plates of salami and eggs. We discussed not only the Suns and the NBA, but really important things like *Seinfeld*, *Curb Your Enthusiasm*, and, one of Al's favorite topics, Johnny Carson. It didn't matter that Al was from a small town in Iowa and I was from Brooklyn. We had in common our love of broadcasting. What's more, Al and I shared the same birthday. What are the odds that both play-by-play announcers from one team were born on the same day?

With the legendary Al McCoy (left) on the night he joined an elite group, the Phoenix Suns' Ring of Honor.

Al retired in 2023 at the age of 90. He spent a mind-boggling fifty-one years behind the Suns mic, touching many generations. Al McCoy will forever be the voice of the Suns.

Al passed away shortly before the release of this book. Aware for years that I was working on it, he asked each time we spoke, "How's the book coming along?" I knew it wasn't going to be published for a while, so in Al's final days, I sent him this story. After reading, he enthusiastically asked for "more, more!" I sent the whole manuscript. After reading the whole thing, he called and said, "What a book . . . what a career . . . a great read!" I thanked Al for his generosity and told him I meant every word of the story about him. That was the last time we talked.

Even though the book wasn't yet in print, I was so happy Al got to enjoy it. I couldn't think of a better way to cap our friendship.

* * *

The date was March 24, 2017. That was the night a twenty-year-old shooting guard for the Phoenix Suns scored 70 points. And the Suns lost.

I was courtside calling that game in Boston when Devin Armani Booker became only the sixth player in NBA history to achieve such greatness. He was also the youngest to do it and he did it against a strong defensive team on the road. The Celtics beat the Suns 130-120 on that fateful night.

The Suns in those days weren't going very far in the standings. There wasn't much to cheer about, except for Devin Booker. The youngster from Grand Rapids, Michigan, who came off the bench as the University of Kentucky's sixth man in his one year there, went on to become a starter and a perennial all-star in the NBA.

What I remember most about that jaw-dropping night was what occurred after the game. In a corridor of the TD Garden, the two team locker rooms were located directly across from each other. In one locker room, there was jubilation. In the other, silence. Remember, Boston won and Phoenix lost but it sounded like the Suns had just captured the NBA championship. Despite another setback, they were celebrating their teammate's astonishing performance. Across the hall, it was like a morgue as the Celtics had let a player light them up for 70 points. Yes, they were victorious but it was a bitter pill to swallow.

Interestingly, when you look at the stats, Booker had 19 points at the half. That's not too shabby but c'mon, nobody was thinking 70. He went on to score 51 points in the second half! My broadcast partner Eddie Johnson, who once scored 43 as a Sun in a second half, saw his franchise record go up in smoke. EJ took it in stride. Finally, Booker's 70 points broke Tom Chamber's team mark of 60 in a game and Tom was also on that telecast as co-host on the pre-game, halftime and post-game shows with Tom Leander in the Suns studio.

There weren't too many highlights during those lean seasons but that night Suns fans could rejoice . . . in defeat.

* * *

In 1950's New York, you lived in a Yankees, Dodgers or Giants household.

Being from Brooklyn, I grew up in a Dodgers family. My father was a Dodgers fan and my brother Marv worked for the Dodgers in their offices at Ebbets Field. My brother Al and I followed suit as Dodger faithful. Being from that borough, rooting for any other local team, especially the Yankees, was considered sacrilegious.

The Dodgers, of course, abandoned Brooklyn and made their Los Angeles debut in 1958. Despite that, my heart remained with the Dodgers.

In the 1960's, pitcher Don Drysdale was my favorite Dodger. Number 53 was a fireballing sidearmer who became a Cy Young Award winner, a three-time World Series champion and a Hall of Famer. I was such an admirer of his, I even imitated his throwing motion when I pitched for my Little League team at Camp Cayuga. That's where any similarity ended. I led the league in hitting batters, often whizzing the ball above and behind campers' ears. Once, I nearly took a kid's head off. I couldn't win a game if my life depended on it, let alone get somebody out.

A Funny Thing Happened on the Way to the Broadcast Booth

Years later, as TV play-by-play announcer for the Phoenix Suns, my broadcast partner, as documented, was former NBA marksman Eddie Johnson. If EJ had to miss a game, the person who took his place was Ann Meyers Drysdale, the wife of the late, great Don Drysdale. It's not often that you get to work closely with the spouse of one of your childhood heroes.

Ann had been a star basketball player at UCLA, an Olympian, the first woman to sign a contract with an NBA team, the Indiana Pacers, and she was one of the first women players inducted into the Basketball Hall of Fame. We're talking basketball royalty.

I must admit, I was nervous before first meeting Ann, but she immediately put me at ease with her infectious smile and engaging personality. I was proud to call her my broadcast partner in my last NBA stop. Today, I'm proud to call her my friend.

It's funny how things sometimes work out that way.

Getting ready to open a Suns broadcast with basketball Hall of Famer Ann Meyers Drysdale (left).

* * *

As if the NBA didn't keep me busy enough in the 1980s, I did television play-by-play for three summers in the World Basketball League on SportsChannel America, a cable television network. It was unique in that players had to be six feet five or under.

The broadcasts were enjoyable thanks primarily to two people. One was good-natured and entertaining on-air cohort Mike Rice, a former college coach who found success behind the mic. The other was experienced producer Steve Danz, a network veteran who produced NFL and MLB games for NBC and ABC, and was one of the best producers I ever worked with.

One game from the WBL really stands out. It took place in Springfield, Illinois, best known for being Abraham Lincoln's final resting place.

About a half hour before airtime, the three of us noticed there was nobody in the stands. Had we hit the air with an empty arena, it would have been embarrassing for the league and for the team owner.

Minutes before tipoff as the national anthem was playing, out of nowhere, people came streaming into the building. Curiously, these folks were on crutches, in wheelchairs, or used canes. Many of them were wearing hospital gowns.

We could only assume that the team had emptied most of the medical facilities in town and somehow hurried everybody to the game in droves. The seats were suddenly full.

I'll say this. As unorthodox as that was, the patients had a blast, wildly cheering on their home team. It was a heartwarming scene and an unforgettable one.

A Funny Thing Happened on the Way to the Broadcast Booth

A Learning Experience

It was my farewell sportscast on the six o'clock news for WCBS-TV Channel 2 in New York. It was 1979, and I had accepted a job as play-by-play announcer for the New York Mets, an opportunity that I couldn't pass up. The TV station thought it would be a neat idea to put my successor, Sal Marchiano, alongside me at the news desk, and I would pass the torch. After my final goodbye, I said, "Now, I'd like to introduce the man who's going to succeed me, well-known New York sportscaster Sal Marchiano. Congratulations Sal, it's all yours." Sal looked at me and said, "Thanks Steve, good luck with the Mets. You'll need it." It was a great line that got a lot of laughs, but unfortunately for me, Sal was right.

I succeeded the legendary Lindsey Nelson, who did play-by-play for the Mets for seventeen years and who was a tough act to follow. Full disclosure: My Mets experience was a wake-up call. While I loved the game, from a broadcasting standpoint, it wasn't in my

A Funny Thing Happened on the Way to the Broadcast Booth

wheelhouse, to borrow a popular baseball term. I was geared toward faster-paced sports, like hockey, basketball, and boxing.

Baseball is a sport of storytelling. Being so young, I hadn't accumulated enough, if any, baseball anecdotes or recollections. As an announcer, that's how you fill the gaps, the lulls, and the many breaks in the game. If you rely only on play-by-play and statistics, your call is apt to be dry and dull. Storytelling is what made Vin Scully so effective. As a storyteller, he had no equal, and the manner in which he wove his stories into his play-by-play was sheer artistry. If that wasn't enough, there are so many nuances and subtleties to the game beneath the surface. Almost like a player, I could have used a few years in the minors to gain experience as a play caller.

After the 1981 season, I was a former Mets announcer. It was the first time in my career I had received this type of gut punch.

From that experience, I learned that we should never stop growing. We evolve as broadcasters, and it doesn't necessarily happen overnight. Sometimes we gain wisdom the hard way. In other words, how can you learn if you don't fail.

What did I do after that? I know it sounds cliché, but I picked myself up and forged ahead with my NBA play-by-play and TV anchoring, and before long, boxing entered my world. Eventually, other exciting facets of the business opened up as well.

The Mets setback didn't dampen my childhood memories of baseball. I'll never forget the time my brother Al and I took the subway to Coogan's Bluff in upper Manhattan. Before moving into their new digs at Shea Stadium in Flushing, Queens in 1964, the Mets played at the old Polo Grounds, vacated by the Giants upon their exit to San Francisco. Al and I were attending a Mets-Dodgers doubleheader. I was about thirteen years old, and Al, four years my senior. Twin bills were the best because we not only got to see two games for the price of one, but we got to spend all day at the ballpark. My mother would pack us sandwiches so we wouldn't have to spend money on stadium food. Today, you'd have to hock your car to afford the concession stands. Anyway, on this day, we got two seats way up in the very last row behind home plate, nosebleed country. It was bliss.

That was the day Jimmy Piersall hit a home run and rounded the bases backwards. Jimmy Piersall was a colorful and controversial ballplayer who overcame mental illness. His rise to the major leagues was depicted in the motion picture *Fear Strikes Out*. He promised to backpedal around the bases after he hit his hundredth career home run, and he kept his word. That scene became baseball folklore, and it was a thrill to see it happen live.

* * *

Pitcher Neil Allen joined the Mets in 1979, when I came on as a broadcaster. He originally came up as a starting pitcher but was then moved to the bullpen. He was a friendly young man with an easy smile out of Kansas City, Kansas.

I remember one time we were talking, and I told him about the former Yankee Ryne Duren who instilled fear in opponents due to his fastball and his thick eyeglasses. Sometimes you never knew where his pitches were going. Like Neil, he was a relief pitcher. I told Neil that there were times when Duren got to the mound, he would go into his warmup motion and fire the ball high over the catcher's head, all the way to the top of the backstop screen, at about ninety-nine miles per hour. Whether he did that intentionally or out of wildness was up for debate, but it always got a rise out of the crowd. The fans loved it. I'm not so sure about the next batter up. Hitters might have thought twice about digging into the batter's box.

Neil seemed to enjoy hearing about Ryan Duren's warmup routine. The next game at Shea Stadium, manager Joe Torre walked out to the mound and signaled for right-hander Neil Allen from the bullpen. Neil trotted to the mound, took the ball from Joe, rubbed it up, then proceeded into his first warmup motion. He fired the ball high over the catcher's head, all the way to the top of the backstop screen at about ninety-nine on the radar gun. The sparse crowd cheered. (There wasn't much to cheer about in those days.) Neil stopped what he was doing, put his hands on his hips and stared straight up at me in the broadcast booth. He was smiling from ear to ear. Somewhere, Ryne Duren had to be smiling too.

* * *

One of the benefits of being on television is that sometimes people will come up to you, offer a nice compliment, and ask for your autograph or a selfie. One time after a Mets game at Shea (way before selfies), I was walking to my car in the parking lot when a gaggle of fans spotted me, then surrounded me and began to stick pens and pieces of paper in my face for my signature. As I was signing the autographs, out of the corner of my eye I saw a guy burrowing his way through the crowd until he finally made his way to the front of the pack.

He was excitedly yelling, "Steve, Steve, Steve."

I kept signing autographs. Then he started jumping up and down and again yelled "Steve, Steve, Steve." I turned to him, expecting an autograph request, and he screeched, "Steve, how do I get to the Whitestone Bridge?"

That is what is known as a humbling experience. Everyone, including me, cracked up.

By the way, just for the record, I gave him directions to the Whitestone Bridge. He said, "Thanks, Steve," and off he went. No autograph request.

Monty, Monty, Monty!

My brother Marv once asked me if I could fill in for him at an awards presentation to be held at a well-known midtown Manhattan hotel. Marv was being honored on this particular night along with other local sports celebrities, but he couldn't be there because he was working. The master of ceremonies for this gala black-tie affair was a onetime announcer for the New York Rangers by the name of Monty Hall, who went on to become the host of a little show called *Let's Make a Deal*.

Public speaking was not my favorite pastime. I had no problem talking sports in front of a camera, but addressing a live audience for any other reason caused heart palpitations. I would sooner get in a ring with the heavyweight champion. Adding to my apprehension, a thousand people were expected. Reluctantly, I bit the bullet and prepared something to say. I couldn't turn down my brother.

A Funny Thing Happened on the Way to the Broadcast Booth

At the reception, they were also presenting an award to a New York area hockey player who was unable to attend because he was playing in a game that night. His wife accepted the award in his place. When she got to the podium, a picture of her husband in his uniform appeared on a giant screen behind her, and she began to cry. She said, "I'm sorry. Whenever I see a picture of my husband in his uniform, I get teary eyed." It was actually very sweet. She went on with her remarks. When she finished, there was a warm round of applause and she went back to her seat at the table.

Monty Hall returned to the microphone to present the next award to Marv. He informed the audience that Marv's brother Steve would be accepting on his behalf. I nervously walked up to the podium to a nice round of applause. Behind me was a large publicity photo of Marv in a suit up on the screen.

I waited for the applause to subside. I gazed over at the picture, pulled out a huge white cloth napkin I had grabbed from my table, and started dabbing my eyes.

I said, "I'm so sorry. Whenever I see a picture of my brother Marv in his suit, I start to cry." The audience erupted with laughter!

I looked to my right, where Monty Hall was standing in the wings near the curtain. He gave me a great big smile and flashed the okay sign with his fingers, the way Johnny Carson used to do to a young standup comedian when he or she crushed it. The instant gratification triggered by the audience response was invigorating. For a fleeting moment, I experienced the high that comedians must feel when they hit it out of the park. But then reality set in. I was a sportscaster who briefly won over a crowd with a wisecrack at an awards banquet.

Knowing the trepidation I had about speaking in front of a live audience, Marv called me later that night at home. Imagine his surprise when I said, "Let me know your next speaking engagement. I'm always available to take your place." Yes, I had discovered the cure for fear of public speaking: a funny opening line.

Punchlines

From an announcing standpoint, boxing was different from mainstream sports. As much preparation as I did, when I called boxing, I sometimes felt as if I was walking on a tightrope without a net. To borrow a boxing term, you had to roll with the punches.

It was a busy time in my life. I was principally doing television play-by-play for New Jersey Nets basketball and sports anchoring on the local news broadcasts in New York. Now I was adding boxing blow-by-blow to my sportscasting repertoire. As I would say on the air, "Welcome to *Showtime Championship Boxing!*"

Friends and acquaintances were intrigued by my connection to prizefighting. On occasion, so was I. It was unquestionably a departure from basketball and hockey. Much of that, I believe, had to do with the people.

Being in boxing was like stepping into an old black-and-white Humphrey Bogart movie. The personalities were unique, to say the least. I found that fighters were unlike any other professional athletes I had ever encountered. Many were products of incomprehensible backgrounds, fiercely tough neighborhoods, ghettos and, in some cases, jungles. Some got into the sport because they were bullied as children. For others, boxing was a means of survival. In many cases, it was an escape from a way of life that most people couldn't even fathom. It was difficult to imagine a parent encouraging his or her son to become a fighter, although it did happen. Aside from the health risks, only a handful make the big money. It's a tough way to earn a living.

Then you had the trainers and cut men. I was not a fan of blood, but watching the cut men work their magic in the corners between rounds was fascinating. They were a special breed who had names like Eddie "The Clot" Aliano and Jacob "Stitch" Duran.

The in-your-face promoters were sometimes more pugilistic than the fighters. The boxing writers were a throwback to a bygone era. The oversized entourages and hangers-on were omnipresent.

Boxing to me as an announcer was an acquired taste and, in terms of its ferocity, clearly in a league of its own. There were times when it felt circus-like with regard to the bluster and taunting at pre-fight press conferences. Often, I found myself shaking my head, and would repeatedly say, on and off the air, "Only in boxing, folks, only in boxing." Almost nothing in sports, however, could equal the electric atmosphere of a world championship fight, or the extraordinary courage of the fighters I consistently witnessed and described. As I became more comfortable with the idiosyncrasies of the sport, I began to understand how boxing had a way of sucking you in, like the undertow of the ocean.

* * *

A good portion of my twenty-plus years at Showtime saw the one and only Don King promoting our fights. Don became an iconic boxing promoter who was just as famous for his hair (he liked to say that it pointed straight up to the heavens) as for his lengthy lectures to hype his fights. He promoted some of the biggest names and mega fights in boxing history, from Muhammad Ali to Mike Tyson, and rose to be one of the most powerful men in the sport.

One time in Las Vegas, Don invited my broadcast partner, Ferdie Pacheco, and me into his business trailer at one of our hotel boxing venues to lend insight, we assumed, on the upcoming fight. Instead, we had a ringside seat to Don's phone conversation with the president of one of the major boxing organizations. The subject matter? Why Don had not been named Promoter of the Year.

The one-way conversation went from a slow burn to a full-blown conflagration. I had never heard such a verbal eruption. Ferdie and I looked at each other in disbelief as the tirade continued. Don's deafening roar was actually scaring me.

After his diatribe died down, Don hung up the phone with a serious look on his face. Then, he let loose with his trademark cackling laugh. He looked at the two of us with a big smile and said, "Guess what? I'm the Promoter of the Year." It was a performance worthy of an Oscar.

* * *

Showtime Championship Boxing took me to many faraway places for broadcasts. In 2001, we had an outdoor telecast at a stadium in Copenhagen, Denmark. In the midst of a steady downpour, favorite son Brian Nielsen walked to the ring to fight Mike Tyson. The Danish fighter joined the sellout crowd in singing Monty Python's "Always Look on the Bright Side of Life." As Nielsen passed by me near our ringside broadcast position, I could hear him belting it out at the top of his lungs. It was one of the more comical ring walks I had ever witnessed. Nielsen and his devoted flock knew the odds, so why not have some fun with it?

As expected, Tyson had his way throughout the fight. He decked Nielsen near the end of round three with a six-punch combination to the head. The Dane went reeling off the ropes and down to the canvas for only the second time in his career. A low blow by Tyson made matters worse, and by the end of the sixth round, Nielsen's left eye, which had been slashed in the second, was completely closed. He didn't answer the bell for round seven, and that was it. While Nielsen managed to go longer than most of Tyson's opponents, he took a beating. Despite fighting on his home turf, in front of his adoring fans, Nielsen knew he was going into a lion's den. The outcome was inevitable, and everyone knew it. He clearly had a sense of humor about it, and the entire crowd rallied around their hometown hero in spirit and in song.

As I was broadcasting in front of a castle in Cardiff, Wales, I was thinking of the line "I'm the king of the castle," uttered by the *Honeymooners'* Ralph Kramden.

* * *

During my years at Showtime, Steve Farhood was primarily the color commentator for *ShoBox: The New Generation,* an offshoot of *Showtime Championship Boxing,* that featured up-and-coming prospects in the ring. Every once in a while, I had the pleasure of working with Steve on our telecasts. He had carved his niche in the fight game as a premier boxing historian and editor-in-chief of *The Ring* and *KO* magazines. I had always considered him a consummate pro on the air, and on one particular night in Glasgow, Scotland, he showed just how unflappable he was.

Hours before this 2003 broadcast, I had chomped on a cookie and a tooth fell out. It was too late to go to a dentist, so I purchased and applied some denture adhesive. I should also point out that the snapped tooth was from the front of my mouth, so you couldn't miss it. I applied the dental glue and made the tooth stick as tightly as I possibly could. Then I prayed to the television gods.

Just before we hit the air, I informed Steve of my mishap. We received our cue to open the broadcast, then just as I turned to Steve to ask him the first question, wouldn't you know it, the tooth came loose again.

I tried to angle my face away from the camera to hide the gap in my mouth. I looked like Alfred E. Neuman, the cartoon cover boy of *Mad* magazine, who famously said "What, me worry?" While Steve answered my question, I manipulated the tooth with my tongue, trying to put it back in place. Steve, very much aware of the situation, tried to keep a straight face. He continued to answer the question without so much as a smirk, and just as he finished, I was somehow able with my tongue to flip the tooth right side up and back where it belonged, then turn my face toward the camera.

To this day, I have no idea how I managed to do it. We got off camera to go to the tale of the tape for the first fight, and I was home free. The fact that Steve was able to keep it together and answer a question on national TV, while standing that close to me and watching my tongue and tooth gymnastics, showed him to be eminently qualified for the International Boxing Hall of Fame.

* * *

I had many favorite fights on *Showtime Championship Boxing*, and near the top of the list has to be Christy Martin vs. Deirdre Gogerty, a blazing six rounds of action in Las Vegas won by Martin. In a sport that is often accused of being hyperbolic, this was aptly labeled the female rendition of the Thrilla in Manila. It gave women's boxing a major boost. Afterward, both fighters were splashed all over the boxing magazines, and Christy made the cover of *Sports Illustrated*, the pinnacle for an athlete.

While the fight was captivating, I'll never forget our prefight meeting with Deidre. She lived in Dublin but was born in an Irish town named Drogheda. I asked her for the pronunciation of her hometown. I said, "Please say it very slowly, so I can be sure to get it right for the TV audience." Without hesitation, she enunciated slowly, "Duuub-lliiinn."

There was a pause, then everyone burst into laughter. But Deidre was serious. She thought I meant Dublin, where she lived, not Drogheda, her place of birth.

Some years later, following her retirement from boxing, I saw Deirdre in the pressroom of another Vegas fight we were covering on Showtime. Our eyes met and we immediately laughed then embraced. No explanation was necessary.

* * *

Another favorite was when two proud warriors, Johnny Tapia and Paulie Ayala, locked horns. Tapia was skillful but liked to entertain the crowd with antics. Both were elite fighters with championship belts. It's traditional for the challenger to walk in first, then the champion. In this case, neither fighter wanted to enter the ring first. Each was adamant about that.

They agreed beforehand to do their ring walks simultaneously. Simultaneously? That was unheard of in boxing. It's just something you never saw.

When the night of the fight arrived and Tapia and Ayala walked toward the ring at the same time, it caught the crowd by surprise. We knew it was coming, but the fans did not. In unison, they walked up their respective steps toward the ring. When they got to the top step, they stopped and looked at each other.

The men then tried to fake each other out in an attempt to get the other to step through the ropes first. Tapia would head fake and lunge forward as if he was about to step into the ring. Then Ayala would do the same. Back and forth they went. The fans, which had now caught on, were delirious with laughter, and so were we.

After several minutes of this folly, the two fighters climbed through the ropes and into the ring, you got it, simultaneously. Interestingly, I don't remember a thing about that fight. Only the ring walks.

* * *

Then there was British heavyweight Julius Francis in Manchester, England. Francis had no chance against Mike Tyson, and he probably figured, "Hey, why not capitalize on the situation?"

To nobody's surprise, Francis was decked five times in the first two rounds. Iron Mike put him flat on his back in the second round and, as Francis was being counted out by the referee, it was hard not to notice that emblazoned on the soles of his shoes were the words "Buy the London Daily Mirror." I can only suppose that the next day newspaper sales in London skyrocketed.

* * *

During my time as a boxing announcer, I shared the broadcast table with some of the leading color commentators in the sport. I'm referring to Ferdie Pacheco, Bobby Czyz, and Al Bernstein. I was also fortunate during my career to work alongside Arthur Mercante, Gil Clancy, Sugar Ray Leonard, Antonio Tarver, Steve Farhood, Randy Gordon, and even Mike Tyson.

My broadcast partners for many years on Showtime were former world champion Bobby Czyz (left) and the famed "Fight Doctor," Ferdie Pacheco (right).

Ferdie Pacheco was one of a kind. The Fight Doctor, as he was better known, was not just any medical doctor. He was Muhammad Ali's personal physician, working in the Greatest's corner for countless historic fights. He was also an accomplished artist and author, a Renaissance man. I learned a lot about boxing just by being around him, observing and listening.

Perhaps the best advice I ever received from Ferdie was early on in my blow-by-blow career: "Always cover your coffee at ringside with an index card, unless you like your coffee with cream, sugar, and blood."

He wrote a book, *Blood in My Coffee*, chronicling his years as a boxing commentator. I carried the Fight Doctor's words of wisdom with me until the end of my fight-calling days, and from force of habit, I always carry index cards with me, in case I go to a coffee shop.

I may have taken Ferdie's advice too far.

Working a boxing telecast with Sugar Ray Leonard (right), one of the all-time greats.

* * *

Nobody could analyze a fight faster or dissect a fighter's skills better than Al Bernstein.

Aside from his boxing acumen, he was one of the most personable and likable people in broadcasting. On top of that, he laughed at my silly jokes.

Al knew of my fascination with Jerry Lewis as a performer. I often imitated Jerry around the Showtime crew. Whenever I would belt out a loud, "Hey LAAAADYYYYYYYY!, it was a surefire way to loosen up fellow commentator Bobby Czyz before a show.

A Funny Thing Happened on the Way to the Broadcast Booth

Prior to one of our Showtime telecasts, I mentioned to Al that the first movie I saw in my life was *At War with the Army*, starring Dean Martin and Jerry Lewis. My mother had taken me to see it when I was about seven years old. Once I saw that, I became a lifelong fan of Jerry. I even had the DVD of that flick.

As it turns out, Al was friends with Jerry Lewis. Al offered to have Jerry sign something for me. I gave him the DVD I had of *At War with the Army*.

I loved working with Al Bernstein (left) on *Showtime Championship Boxing* because he laughed at my jokes. He was also an excellent TV boxing analyst.

Well, a month later, prior to our next broadcast, he gave the DVD back to me. There was nothing written on it, no Jerry Lewis autograph. Then he reached into his briefcase and came out with an old VHS tape of *At War with the Army* still in the box. It was signed by Jerry Lewis. Jerry told Al that there was nowhere on the DVD he could sign his name, so he grabbed a VHS tape from his own personal stash. On the outside cardboard holder, he wrote, "For Steve, from Jerry Lewis."

Jerry, I learned, didn't do that for everybody but Al told me he watched us all the time and was a fan. To someone like myself who was still a kid at heart, that meant a lot and I'll always be thankful to Al Bernstein for that.

* * *

Jim Gray was our intrepid ringside reporter on *Showtime Championship Boxing*. He always knew where to find controversy, or it found him.

Jim had a playful but devilish side to him that not too many people knew about. When I wasn't looking, he would hide my meticulously prepared notes minutes before we went on the air, which always almost gave me heart failure. Jim, I forgive you.

In 2018, as fate would have it, Jim and I were inducted into the same International Boxing Hall of Fame class. Remembering what Jim used to do to me before shows, I locked my Hall of Fame speech in the hotel room vault, then kept it as far away from him as possible before I stepped up to the podium to accept the honor. I also made two extra copies, placing one in each of my jacket pockets. I wasn't taking any chances.

A Funny Thing Happened on the Way to the Broadcast Booth

The Bite Fight and Other Chunks of Boxing History

By and large, Showtime aired major marquee fights. They were televised live to a national audience. They did not come much bigger than the pay-per-view event of Holyfield vs. Tyson II for the WBA Heavyweight Championship.

The buildup to the rematch between Evander "The Real Deal" Holyfield and "Iron Mike" Tyson on June 28, 1997, was enormous, particularly following Holyfield's stunning upset in the first fight, a riveting eleventh round technical knockout victory for the title. That stirring win propelled Holyfield to legendary status.

A Funny Thing Happened on the Way to the Broadcast Booth

Boxing and controversy go together and the sequel was no exception. It was delayed six weeks by a Tyson injury, capped by a last-minute switch of referees due to a Team Tyson protest.

Most performers of any type—actor or announcer—usually report having preshow jitters. After years of announcing, I still got nervous before a broadcast, especially the big ones.

In the days and weeks leading up to such fights, my stomach would pay the price. It would be tied up in knots, and I'd be popping Tums into my mouth like Tic Tacs. Once a fight started, however, I fell into to the familiarity of the blow-by-blow routine, and I was able to control any jitters I might have had.

I wasn't struck by nerves as much doing play-by-play of other sports, like basketball and hockey. Those games were broadcast on an almost daily basis, and there was not much time to think between games. You just got up to the mic and performed. Mega fights did not happen regularly. There was a lot of time between those fights, a lot of time to think about how things could go wrong.

On the night of the rematch, I had more butterflies than usual. I was always uneasy before calling a Mike Tyson fight. He was so unpredictable. You just never knew what to expect from the guy. Generally, for any fight, I would prepare scrupulously. I would research each fighter's background, study tapes, talk to as many people as possible, and gather as much information as I could. I always prepared extensive notes. For each broadcast, I might refer to only about ten percent of my notes, but it made me feel better psychologically to be well prepared.

For Tyson, I expected him to engage in disruptive antics for which no amount of traditional pre-fight preparation would cover (such as a fighter's style, hand speed or defensive skills). I would have to wing that part of the broadcast. Accordingly, that night, despite my thorough preparation, the butterflies were doing cartwheels in my stomach.

My heart was pounding and my apprehension building as I took the long walk from my room at the MGM Grand Hotel Casino in Las

Vegas to the MGM Grand Garden Arena to get ready to call that busy night of boxing that would culminate with the much-publicized, highly-anticipated main event.

I weaved through the immense crowds, lugging my bulky briefcase stuffed with scripts and endless notes, navigating through and around masses of people in the smoke-filled casino. I heard the ding-ding-ding of the rows and rows of slot machines, cheers ringing out intermittently from the craps tables, and the steel balls rolling around the roulette wheels. The cacophony was overwhelming. In Vegas, it didn't seem to matter what time of day it was—morning, afternoon, or night, bright sunshine or total darkness outside, those sights and sounds never changed.

In this case, the commotion level was more intense and the crowds larger, with boxing fans mixing in with the regular casino patrons. The game plan was working—the hotel nabs a big fight, and more customers flock there to gamble.

While surrounded by this hullabaloo, I remember thinking to myself that Tyson was going to do something unusual that night. Of course, that would be nothing new but I had this sinking feeling in my gut that he was going to pull something exceedingly out of the ordinary. His grousing about Holyfield's head butts in the first fight added to my concern.

Nobody could have foreseen what actually happened. I had a hunch, but I had no idea what specifically Tyson was going to do. Had I opened that broadcast with "Folks, tonight I predict that Mike Tyson will bite off a chunk of Evander Holyfield's ear," some fellas in white coats might have approached me and said, "Uh, Steve, could you come with us, please?"

The main event began. Holyfield picked up where he had left off in the first fight. He started strong in the first two rounds, but, as in the first bout, their heads were colliding. Tyson sustained a cut over his right eye. Little did we know how much those Holyfield head butts had irritated him.

With about forty seconds left in round three, the two fighters got into a clinch.

That's when things took a wild and unforgettable turn as Tyson gnawed off the top of Holyfield's right ear.

Initially, from my angle at ringside, I could not see the bite. When Holyfield grabbed his ear and started hopping around, I said, "What's going on here? Holyfield, jumping up and down!" He was in obvious distress.

Then, in horror, I shouted, "Oh my goodness, he's got a bloody right ear! Holyfield bit by a dirty Mike Tyson!" I could not believe what I was seeing, or saying, and suddenly I was flying by the seat of my pants.

With blood gushing from Holyfield's ear, horror turned to shock. This was something I had never before experienced behind a mic. How does one prepare for it? There's no playbook for such an occurrence. Flashing through my mind was that I had been right about Tyson pulling a bizarre stunt, but biting off a piece of Holyfield's ear was not on my list of potential Tyson shenanigans. Following the bite, Tyson charged Holyfield from the rear and pushed him into his corner.

The fight was paused as referee Mills Lane conferred with Mark Ratner, head of the Nevada Athletic Commission along with ringside physician Flip Homansky. Stopping the fight after the bite might have triggered huge problems. I had experienced my fair share of spectator uprisings as a blow-by-blow announcer, and, given the high stakes, this had the potential to be the mother of all ring riots. The crowd of more than 16,000 was getting anxious.

Apparently, Lane was ready to disqualify Tyson, but Dr. Homansky said that Holyfield could continue. There was a collective sigh of relief in the arena. Bite or no bite, the fans had come to see a fight.

Lane did deduct two points from Tyson. When he explained that to Tyson, Mike insisted that Holyfield's ear injury came from a punch. "Bulls--t," said Mills Lane.

The fight resumed and just moments later, I blurted, "He bit him again! Mike Tyson has bitten Evander Holyfield for the second time and it is all-out war!" This time, Tyson targeted the left ear, and there was more blood. Lane did not immediately stop the fight because he didn't see the second bite. The two men continued to battle until the bell sounded. Tyson and Holyfield went back to their corners, at which time it was determined that a second bite had occurred. The fight was at a standstill again.

Within seconds, the ring was flooded with local police and MGM Grand Garden security. Arena enforcement encircled Holyfield in his corner. Then, Tyson started swinging indiscriminately and all hell broke loose. I yelled, "Tyson is just taking swipes at anybody in front of him. It's a fiasco." Pandemonium reigned.

Meantime, Tyson's corner was informed by Lane that their fighter was disqualified. Lane said he warned Tyson not to bite Holyfield again, and when he did, Lane DQ'd Tyson for intentional bites.

When Holyfield left the ring, it was a pretty good tip-off to the fans and those watching on TV that the fight was over, but there was no official announcement for another twenty-five minutes.

In the midst of the confusion and craziness, I tried to maintain my composure on the air. As the situation grew even more chaotic, I reminded myself to just describe what was going on, as a reporter would. I managed to get through the debacle and the broadcast. I couldn't wait to get out of there and return to the quiet of my room. As soon as we dropped the microphones, I was gone.

Normally, after shows I would stay around and engage in post-fight banter with my broadcast partners, check with the production truck to see how everything went, or grab a bite (no pun intended).

This night, I was not in the mood for pleasantries. When I went up the escalator to exit the arena, all I could see was a mob scene. There was no way out except for the way I came in, through a long corridor of shops and restaurants that led to the casino. It was wall-to-wall humanity. Somehow, I bulldozed my way through the throng, using my bulky briefcase almost as a battering ram. I tried to be polite, but I was terse with those who wanted my take on what we had just witnessed.

The din of the casino was getting closer. I finally made it to the rows of elevators in the lobby. It took forever it seemed for the doors to open, and when they did, another crush of people poured out to go gamble into the night or party into the morning.

I made it to my room, which might have been in another zip code it was so far from the elevators. I frantically fished through my pockets for the key. When I got inside, I didn't even turn on the lights. The room was pitch black, and the silence was such a relief from all the tumult. There was calm.

My briefcase dropped from my hand to the floor. Still wearing my full tuxedo, complete with dried blood droplets on my jacket and shirt offering me gruesome souvenirs of my evening, I collapsed on my back onto the bed. Lying there in the darkness, I stared up at the ceiling, my head spinning.

I remember asking myself, "What in God's name just happened?" I jokingly thought, "I don't recall covering this in Broadcasting 101." Maybe I had been absent that day. You know, the day the professor taught the class how to announce an event in which somebody bites off a piece of an opponent's ear.

Years later, at my Boxing Hall of Fame induction weekend, where Tyson was on hand, he had noticeably mellowed and could not have been more gracious. In fact, during an interview session for the fans, he even joked about that notorious night. At the start of round three, Mills Lane had ordered Tyson back to his corner because he didn't have his mouthpiece in. I asked Mike if he had done that deliberately, with the intent to bite Holyfield. He said to me, "Nah, those dum-dums in my corner forgot to put it back in my mouth."

Close to two million people tuned in to see Holyfield vs. Tyson II in 1997. To this day, it is still the number two all-time viewership for a pay-per-view boxing event, behind only the Floyd Mayweather-Oscar De La Hoya bout in 2005, which had 2.4 million buys.

At his Monday press conference following the fight, in the midst of countless world events and crises, the first question reporters asked President Bill Clinton was "Mr. President, did you see the fight?" The President said, "Yes, I saw it, and I was horrified." I thought, "Thank goodness, he wasn't referring to the broadcast."

Holyfield-Tyson II instantly became synonymous with the word infamous. Originally called "The Sound and the Fury," it will forever be known as "The Bite Fight." One of the strangest chapters in boxing history was undoubtedly the most memorable and challenging night of my broadcasting career.

* * *

"The only reason Chavez was 84-0 was because he fought Tijuana taxi drivers that my mom could whip!"
— Greg Haugen

I had never seen so many people in one place at the same time—132,247 spectators. It was mind-blowing to look out over this sea of humanity, all there to see one man beat the daylights out of another. The quote at the top of this story? Let's just say it didn't hurt the attendance.

The scene was Azteca Stadium in Mexico City. To call this outdoor arena colossal is an understatement. It felt like five Yankee Stadiums could fit inside it. Normally, it was used as a soccer venue. On this night, it was home to *El Gran Campeón*. That's right, Mexico's treasured jewel, the great boxing champion Julio César Chávez.

This is the story, not so much about the fighter, but of the number of people who came to see him fight. I was there to provide the commentary from ringside for *Showtime Championship Boxing*.

Chávez, of course, was wildly popular south of the border. He was the World Boxing Council super lightweight champion at the time, undefeated, with that staggering record of 84-0. He was thirty years of age when this fight took place, and in many minds the best pound-for-pound fighter in the world. He was punishing in the ring, and his ferocity was unquestioned. He seemed destined to win a hundred fights without a loss.

His opponent on this night was a former lightweight and junior welterweight titlist from Auburn, Washington, named Greg Haugen. Despite those championship belts, he wasn't in the same category as Chávez. Not only that, Haugen was now thirty-two years old, on the other side of the boxing mountain.

Do you actually think promoter Don King would put Chávez in there with a guy who could pose a legitimate threat on a night like this? It was difficult to find anybody who thought that Greg Haugen was going to throw a wrench into Chávez's plans to stay undefeated.

Don't get me wrong, Haugen was one hard-nosed dude. That's what made it enticing. He had a reputation for fighting in bars, and earlier in his career, he had fought in "tough guy" competitions. There was no doubting his grit in the ring.

The fight that night was not about pitting evenly matched boxers against each other, it was about filling the stadium. There is always a bit of in-your-face machismo acted out in sporting events. Some of it is just good old-fashioned trash talking. Other times, the smack talk is a promotional gimmick.

Don King would stop at nothing to publicize one of his fights.

He may even have encouraged Haugen to fill the seats by insulting the hometown champion to rile up the local fans. Haugen undermined Chávez's winning record by first characterizing his opponents as mere Tijuana taxi drivers, later saying, "Look at Chávez's first fifty fights. If you recognize those names, you're a boxing historian. They're nothing but palookas. Am I supposed to be scared?"

If that wasn't enough fuel in the fire, he added, "There are not even one hundred thirty thousand Mexicans who could afford a ticket to the fight." That was some serious smack, and his incendiary words clearly got under people's skins.

Well, the stars aligned, and on the night of the fight, spectators showed up in droves. The official count was 132,247, but some said there were 136,000 people there. As I looked around from my broadcast table at ringside, it was surreal. The attendance shattered the previous record of 120,470 for the Jack Dempsey vs. Gene Tunney heavyweight title fight that took place in Philadelphia in 1926.

When you think about all the momentous championship fights through the years, it's curious that Chávez vs. Haugen holds the attendance record. Don King knew an angle when he saw one, and in this case, it was national pride.

Given the gargantuan crowd, I remember hoping things wouldn't get out of control, as had happened in the past in Mexico. If the Bite Fight could have been the mother of all ring riots, this could have become the mother-in-law of all boxing riots.

Security was tight, with barbed wire around the stadium's fencing. There seemed to be thousands of police armed with Uzis, some with trained German shepherds held tightly on leashes. The organizers had added a moat around the ring. I would not have been surprised if there were alligators in the moat.

Haugen, as the challenger, entered first, carrying an American flag. His ring walk music was Bruce Springsteen's "Born in the USA." As you might expect, Haugen was showered with boos. When Chávez made his entrance, he was awarded with an explosion of applause. His ring walk music seemed to be the cheers of the crowd. The noise was deafening. After the instructions by referee Joe Cortez, Chávez refused to touch gloves. The crowd erupted into louder cheers of approval.

The champion was known to start his fights in deliberate fashion. This night, he made an exception. Chávez wanted to punish Haugen from the opening bell.

A Funny Thing Happened on the Way to the Broadcast Booth

The monstrous crowd was thrilled that their hero was making Haugen pay for his disrespectful words. As the fight unfolded, it became quite evident that it was no contest. It did not appear to be heading to a controversial decision, a relief to us at ringside and I'm sure to the vast security force.

Chávez was relentless, and his signature left hooks to the body and vicious combinations took their toll on Haugen. The challenger had pluck, but he was now damaged goods, and the merciless beating was stopped in round five.

After the fight, Chávez said that Haugen deserved to be punished for the things he said in the fight buildup. In the words of Chávez, "Now you know I don't fight with taxi drivers." I give Haugen credit, as his response was quite witty: "They must have been tough taxi drivers."

We remember most fights because of what happened *inside* the ring. In the case of Chávez vs. Haugen, it's what occurred *outside* the ring that was positively remarkable. There are 132,247 reasons why.

* * *

Of the 300-plus world championship fights I announced on Showtime, one stands out as the most exciting and dramatic. It took place on May 7, 2005, at the Mandalay Bay in Las Vegas. In all my years of broadcasting boxing, it was undeniably the most compelling prizefight I ever had the privilege of describing. It was one of the most breathtaking and heart pounding battles in boxing history, and some pundits went so far as to say it was the greatest fight of all time. It definitely was the fight of the year.

Diego "Chico" Corrales took on José Luis Castillo to unify the World Boxing Organization and WBC lightweight titles. It certainly had the elements of a combative fight, but to say that it exceeded expectations is a massive understatement.

The lanky Corrales, bustling with personality and charisma, was the WBO champion, out of Sacramento, California. The more stoic and businesslike Castillo, known for ripping vicious left hooks, possessed the WBC belt and hailed from Empalme, Sonora, Mexico. He was another in a long line of fierce champions from south of the border.

Adding even more clout to the contest was that it took place on the weekend of the Boxing Writers Association of America's annual dinner in Sin City. With so many media members in attendance, the fight received more coverage than it might have otherwise.

Even before the fight began, one of the factors that made it so intriguing was that historically, Corrales never went by the book. He took risks. In this case, he decided to hook with the hooker. That's usually a mistake, but Corrales made it work. It was a questionable strategy against a tremendous body puncher, but I think that despite his knowing Corrales's reputation, Castillo was surprised that he took that tack. It certainly made for huge fireworks.

There was phenomenal back and forth action throughout. Neither fighter budged an inch. The crowd was into the action right from the opening bell, and each round was absolutely gripping. Corrales chose to fight fire with fire, which translated to an astounding slugfest. It may have been an uncertain game plan, but it made for spellbinding television. Everyone—the combatants, the crowd, and all of us at ringside—was locked in.

It was ten rounds of sheer mayhem. Both guys gave and took hellacious shots. As the two-way beating raged on, Corrales's and Castillo's faces and bodies were battered and bruised.

Castillo was cut over his left eye. Both of Corrales's eyes were badly swollen and by the seventh round his left eye was barely a slit. I don't know how he could see out of it. With all the punishment dished out, that a knockdown never occurred through the first nine rounds was astonishing.

Then came the tenth, the round that transformed the fight into an instant classic. I had never announced anything like that in my career. Less than thirty seconds in, Corrales absorbed a sharp punch to the chin. He hit the canvas. It was the first knockdown of the fight.

Corrales was gasping for air, so he spit out his mouthpiece. The referee, Tony Weeks, counted, "one, two, three, four, five, six, seven . . . ." Corrales made it to his feet on the count of eight. Then, just like that, Corrales was on the deck again, knocked down twice in a matter of seconds in the tenth round. Out came Corrales' mouthpiece again. This time, he managed to stand up at the count of nine. He was that close to losing right there. To add insult to injury, Weeks took a point away from Corrales for excessively spitting his mouthpiece out. Castillo continued to land ferocious blows.

It appeared hopeless to almost everyone in the arena and I'm sure to most watching on TV. How much more beating could Corrales take? He seemed to have nothing left in the tank.

Then, as if by magic, it happened. In the blink of an eye, the tide turned. Corrales landed what Castillo would later call "a perfect right hand." Corrales then pinned Castillo against the ropes and connected with a series of resounding punches that rocked Castillo to the core. Corrales hurt Castillo with an explosive left hook. From there, he poured it on with monstrous shots to the head. At that point, the ref had seen enough and stopped the fight.

The fans in the Mandalay Bay Arena, who were cheering nonstop, were now beside themselves. They knew they had just witnessed a fight for the ages. Diego Corrales had been on the verge of being knocked out, dropped not once but twice in the tenth round. Yet he somehow came back to win, and he did it in dramatic fashion.

I saw it firsthand and still cannot believe what happened. To be there, to witness that event live, was about as electrifying as it gets in the sport of boxing. To be the one calling it on television? It's difficult to describe how exhilarating that was.

To this day, I do not know how Diego Corrales summoned up the reserve, the will, and the fortitude to win that fight. He took heart, determination, and competitive drive to inconceivable heights. Okay, there was some controversy, but when has there not been controversy in boxing? Corrales may have been given extra time to retrieve his mouthpiece. Some thought the stoppage may have been premature.

When you study the tape, you see what a discerning job referee Tony Weeks did in managing that fight. His willingness to not interfere and let them fight allowed Corrales and Castillo to take the term "Ring Warriors" to a new level.

Afterwards, the fight gained so much acclaim and attention, it garnered its own page on Wikipedia, complete with a quote of my call at the end of the fight.

> Unbelievable ebb and flow! They're all standing here at Mandalay Bay! Corrales coming back after being on the canvas twice here in the tenth! Now, Castillo steps back! Corrales winging! Castillo's in trouble! Weeks steps in, and the fight . . . is . . . over! Corrales with a remarkable, dramatic turnaround to win this fight! Unbelievable! Diego Corrales said he would go through hell before losing this fight! He may have.

My broadcast partner, Al Bernstein, astutely added, "That might be the single most extraordinary comeback within a round to win a fight that has ever happened."

Naturally, a brawl like that begged a rematch. However, like so many sequels, it didn't live up to the original. Castillo didn't make weight, and it was deemed a nontitle affair. The bloom was off the rose. They fought again, but it wasn't the same. They exchanged punches from the get-go as in the first fight, but this one ended with a thud as Corrales got tagged with a left hook to the chin in round four, and that's where it ingloriously ended. Corrales struggled to his feet as the referee counted to ten, and Castillo evened the score. They scheduled a third fight, but it never happened, with weight again the issue.

Corrales would never win another fight. On May 7, 2007, two years to the day after their first encounter, Diego Corrales lost his life in a motorcycle accident. Jose Luis Castillo went on to fight until 2014, when he finally called it quits.

Corrales vs. Castillo. A fight like that happens only once in a lifetime, and I was lucky enough to call it.

Boxing's Highest Honor

As I was standing behind a podium getting ready to speak, I looked out onto the enormous crowd. Sitting right in front of me were Julius Erving, Larry Fitzgerald, and Bob Costas. Seated behind me were Mike Tyson, Marvin Hagler, and Thomas Hearns.

It felt like a dream as I was being inducted into the International Boxing Hall of Fame. If only my father could have been there on that sun-drenched Sunday afternoon in Canastota, New York. The date was June 10, 2018.

It is said that going into a Hall of Fame is a validation of many years of hard work but such occasions embarrassed me. Deep down, it's not what I'm about. The opening line of my speech was, "Before we go any further, let me just ask, are you sure you've got the right Albert?"

A Funny Thing Happened on the Way to the Broadcast Booth

* * *

I became an announcer because I loved broadcasting. All I ever wanted to be was a sportscaster. I didn't always get it right but I tried to do my job with honesty and integrity. I was fortunate to grow up in a broadcasting family. I've never taken that for granted. My brothers and I all had the same dream. We achieved our dreams with desire, drive and dedication.

Each of my brothers called boxing at different points in their careers. I made my boxing broadcasting debut in 1984 calling the action for a show called *Super Fights of the Month* on SportsChannel America. The late boxing promoter Dan Duva, who helmed Main Events, gave me my first break in boxing by recommending me for the job.

It seemed that Dan's family and relatives were all involved in the boxing world. Main Events boxers were trained by Dan's dad, the legendary Lou Duva. Dan's first cousins, brothers Frank and Rick Belmont, were the producers of *Super Fights of the Month*. The Duvas and the Belmonts grew up together and their homes were next to each other. Today the company is run by Dan's wife, Kathy Duva.

My broadcast partner was fabled boxing referee Arthur Mercante, whom I immediately dubbed "The Illustrious Arthur Mercante" because he carried himself with such class and dressed impeccably. I think Arthur and I were the only ones with Main Events who weren't related.

In 1987, Jim Spence, a longtime TV executive, who wrote the iconic book *Up Close & Personal*, gave me the opportunity to become Showtime's blow-by-blow announcer. Jay Larkin would become Senior Vice President and Executive Producer of *Showtime Championship Boxing* and he helped me grow as a boxing commentator.

Thanks to all those people, I had the honor of calling some of the biggest fights in boxing history for over a quarter of a century.

At Showtime we had a devoted production team led by producer David Dinkins Jr. The VP of Production was Gordon Hall. Both were seasoned pros. Our live telecasts and pre-production work, by colleagues such as Earl Fash and Jody Heaps, were a source of tremendous pride to all involved. Everyone who worked for *Showtime Championship Boxing* and Main Events was a major part of the reason I was in Canastota.

* * *

My induction into the prestigious International Boxing Hall of Fame was most unexpected and, despite my aversion to the spotlight, it was difficult not to get swept up in all the hoopla.

Former heavyweight champion Mike Tyson (right) attended the induction ceremonies. Do you really think he needed that name tag to identify himself?

It seems like the entire boxing world descends upon the modest village of Canastota, New York, about 25 miles east of Syracuse, for this annual event. Only 3.3 miles in size, Canastota has a population of about 4,500 people. Every June it opens its arms and hearts with a festive celebration of boxing's latest Hall of Fame inductees.

Hordes of exuberant fans were on hand, seeking selfies, autographs, and conversation with anybody and everybody associated with the sport. Many camped out in front of the event hotel day and night.

I was fortunate to be included in a talented Hall of Fame class with former world champions Vitali Klitschko, Erik Morales, and Winky Wright, my former Showtime colleague Jim Gray, and promoter Klaus-Peter Kohl. Posthumous inductees included 1920s lightweight star Sid Terris, known as the "Galloping Ghost of the Ghetto," legendary ring announcer Johnny Addie and promoter Lorraine Chargin.

The 2018 International Boxing Hall of Fame Class (from left, Winky Wright, me, Vitali Klitschko, Jim Gray, and Erik Morales).

"Dr. Ironfist," as Klitschko was known, is a former heavyweight champ who entered politics and became mayor of Kyiv, Ukraine. He invited his fellow inductees to his beautiful city. Four years after being inducted, Vitali was valiantly defending his native land from

Russian attack. He seemed so happy when we were all in Canastota, and so proud to be inducted. His younger brother, former heavyweight champ Wladimir Klitschko, was by his side at the Hall of Fame. Later, his brother was by his side in Ukraine's resistance to Russia.

There were many boxing celebrities and sports luminaries in attendance, like former heavyweight contender Gerry Cooney. Gentleman Gerry has a tremendous sense of humor, but I wouldn't recommend getting in a car with him behind the wheel. We caught a ride with Cooney to a Hall of Fame event, held on tightly, and thankfully survived in one piece. It was the first time I got to spend some quality time with him and he won me over with his wit and personality.

With basketball icon Julius Erving (left) at the International Boxing Hall of Fame weekend. Years earlier, I had the honor of emceeing "Dr. J Night" at the Meadowlands Arena.

Gerry was joined by his Sirius XM radio partner Randy Gordon, the ex-New York State Athletic Commissioner and a former broadcast partner of mine. Randy and I did some fights together on

ESPN and were ringside to call boxing for Ted Turner's *Goodwill Games* on TBS in 1990. In Canastota, Randy was never without his trusty tape recorder and was able to score some insightful interviews with boxing celebs for his popular talk show *At the Fights*. One of the sport's good guys, Randy was elected to the Hall of Fame's Class of 2025.

As mentioned, Canastota is a small town and did not have many spare buildings to house the many events held throughout the four-day Hall of Fame celebration. Event organizers used a local funeral home as a staging area for the inductees about to participate in the Parade of Champions. All the inductees and boxing luminaries sat around inside the funeral parlor, on folding chairs, while waiting to board their assigned parade vehicles.

Waving to the crowd at the "Parade of Champions" during the Hall of Fame weekend.

The parade though was anything but funereal. Thousands of townspeople lined the streets on a radiantly beautiful blue-sky day. They waved and cheered as our cars slowly drove down the parade route. We all waved back, sitting on the tops of the back seat of these convertible cars. I rode in style in a gorgeous tan Bentley. The spectacle was classic Americana.

The Banquet of Champions produced another lasting memory. As an inductee, I was tasked with giving a speech. I wanted to be entertaining. At the lectern, I hit the crowd with a series of boxing themed one-liners.

I opened with a couple of jabs:

- "In a Showtime fighter meeting, I once asked a fighter for a prediction of how his fight was going to go. He said, 'I'll knock him out in the first or second round. Whichever comes first.'"
- "Then there was the time I asked a veteran trainer about his fighter's training habits. He said, 'Steve, he's a guy who gets up at five o'clock in the morning, regardless of what time it is.'"

Then, I threw a left hook to the body: "I once asked another trainer if his fighter worked out every day. He said, 'Yes, in fact just yesterday he was on the treadmill for an hour. Then some nincompoop turned it on.'"

And pow! A haymaker to the head: "I once asked a fighter if he was happily married? He said, 'Yes, but my wife's not.'"

Thankfully, the crowd was in a good mood and actually laughed at my attempts at humor.

To me, the best feeling in the world was looking over at Marvelous Marvin Hagler and seeing his reaction. He was howling. When I finished, I walked by him to get back to my seat on the dais. He stopped me and grabbed my arm. He said, "Steve, I didn't realize you were so funny." In a weekend that overflowed with special moments, that might have been the "knockout punch."

A Funny Thing Happened on the Way to the Broadcast Booth

Boxing legend "Marvelous" Marvin Hagler (middle) was among the many luminaries at my Hall of Fame ceremony. Here he was posing with Jim Gray (left) and me.

* * *

When you become a member of the Boxing Hall of Fame, you gain a new family. I was delighted to see so many well-deserving friends get inducted into the family, I mean, the Hall of Fame, through the years. They included noted boxing writer Tom Hauser, who wrote some of the most seminal books on Muhammad Ali, and former Showtime colleagues Al Bernstein, Jim Gray, Steve Farhood and Jimmy Lennon Jr.

I may have to invite them to my next Thanksgiving dinner.

* * *

I was honored to achieve the "hat trick" of boxing inductions by also being accepted into the World Boxing Hall of Fame in 2007 and the New York State Boxing Hall of Fame in 2019.

The World Boxing Hall of Fame event, which was held in Ontario, California, had a special meaning as it was my first hall of fame induction—and most "culinary."

At the ceremony, I was so consumed with presenting a thoughtful speech and conversing with my fellow inductees on the dais that I never had time to eat the meal served at this gala affair. A good friend of mine, Mike Nelson, a former Golden State Warriors public relations man who became the Senior Vice President of Communications at CBS Television, attended the festivities. Upon learning that I had not eaten a morsel of food, Mike decided I needed to be fed.

Following the event, Mike led me to an unforgettable foodie experience that became one of my fondest memories from that night. California natives would appreciate this fact: I had my first "In & Out Burger." It was a revelation. Ask for the "animal style" burger and thank me later.

A Funny Thing Happened on the Way to the Broadcast Booth

I'm Ready for My Close-Up

The biggest movie I ever appeared in was *I Spy*, released in 2002. It's a buddy spy comedy directed by former *Hill Street Blues* star Betty Thomas, who also directed Howard Stern's *Private Parts*. *I Spy* starred Eddie Murphy and Owen Wilson. Eddie played an international spy who goes undercover as a prizefighter. My Showtime broadcast partner, former light heavyweight and cruiserweight champion Bobby Czyz, and I were hired to play ourselves as the ringside announcers.

Bobby and I were tapped to be on camera for a major boxing scene being filmed in Vancouver, British Columbia. They sent us our scripts, and both of us memorized everything word for word.

On the day of shooting, Betty Thomas greeted us with a big smile and told us the reason she had brought us in for this movie was that she was a boxing fan and watched us all the time on Showtime. She wanted the genuine articles to play these roles.

She asked, "Guys, you know the scripts we sent you?"

"Yes!"

"Have you studied your lines?"

"We sure did."

She then said, "Good, I want you to tear everything up. Throw away the script. I just want you to react to what you see. Announce what's in front of you, just like you do on television. That's why we brought you here."

Our jaws dropped. After all that studying and memorizing. Sure, we had called hundreds of fights without a script, but this was a major motion picture starring Eddie Murphy.

Loaded with confidence when we arrived, Bobby and I were suddenly gripped by uncertainty.

We didn't want to hold up the project. The movie had a $70 million budget, and we felt a gigantic weight on our shoulders.

Just then, Eddie Murphy, decked out in his flashy fighter's garb, bounced up the steps and into the ring to get ready for his boxing scene. I had never seen Eddie in person before, only in movies and on TV. Right in front of me was this show business and film icon, the *Saturday Night Live* legend who had starred in box office megahits like *Beverly Hills Cop*, *Trading Places* and *Coming to America*.

Eddie glanced over and spotted us sitting at ringside. He smiled broadly, and his eyes lit up as if he had recognized two long-lost friends.

He darted over from the other side of the ring, leaned through the ropes to shake our hands, and gave Bobby and me a warm welcome. Then he grabbed the PA microphone with his boxing gloves and introduced us to the thousands of extras who made up the crowd. He gave us a beautiful buildup, telling everyone how thrilled he was to have the two of us in the movie, how they were so happy to bring in real live professional boxing announcers from *Showtime* in the U.S. to call the action, and then he said to the crowd, "How about a big round of applause for Steve Albert and Bobby Czyz." We were stupefied. Here was Eddie Murphy, the star of the movie, stopping everything to say hello. He could not have been more gracious, immediately putting us at ease and lifting our spirits.

Bobby and I looked at each other as if to say "Let's do this!" Like Betty Thomas said, we would call it the way we saw it, just like on television. We were psyched.

We announced that boxing scene and all the subsequent fight scenes as if we were ringside calling the action for *Showtime Championship Boxing*, but with a little extra flair. After all, this was the movies.

When Betty yelled "Action," we were One-Take Steve and Bobby. It all turned out great and sounded authentic, just as Betty had envisioned. Afterward, we received a rousing ovation from the thousands of extras in the stands, who all heard our fight calls. Bobby and I were so sky high, we didn't need an airplane for the flight back home.

* * *

Cast as ringside announcers, Steve Farhood and I spent several days on the set of *Lights Out*, a nighttime drama series about a boxer that aired on FX. On these shoots, you find yourself snacking more than usual, thanks to craft services, one of the fringe benefits that compensate for all the waiting around. In addition, the production provides hearty meals throughout the day. If I became a full-time actor, I would probably balloon to three hundred pounds.

One early morning, when Steve and I arrived at the humongous Steiner Studios in Brooklyn, we had nothing but breakfast on our minds. The buffet looked like something you'd see on a Norwegian Cruise Line ship, such as scrambled eggs, pancakes, French toast, bagels, muffins, and fruit.

After stuffing our faces, we stood up and noticed that the people sitting around us didn't look familiar. Not only that, but they were wearing costumes that had nothing to do with boxing.

A Funny Thing Happened on the Way to the Broadcast Booth

We had accidentally stumbled onto the set of *Mildred Pierce*, which was shooting right next door to *Lights Out*. It was a TV miniseries starring Kate Winslet based on the 1945 Joan Crawford movie. We discovered that *Mildred Pierce*'s breakfasts were phenomenal, better than the food we had on our set.

Every morning from that point on, we found ourselves "accidentally" wandering over to *Mildred Pierce* for our daily breakfast. Sshhh. Don't tell anyone, especially Mildred Pierce. If you saw the movie, you know what she's capable of doing. If you didn't see it, spoiler alert: It was murder.

* * *

I was behind the mic for memorable episodes of some situation comedies. The first sitcom relates to this sports trivia question: What three members of the same family have announced for the New York Knicks? If you said, Marv, Kenny, and Steve Albert, you're right. My brother Marv was the longtime voice of the Knicks. My nephew Kenny backs up Mike Breen on Knicks telecasts. And, I once played the role of the Knicks announcer in the long-running HBO hit series, *Sex and the City*. It was a trick question.

The episode, which first aired in 1999, was entitled "Games People Play." I like to tell people that my co-star on this episode was Jon Bon Jovi, but that's kind of a reach. Bon Jovi played a fellow who keeps running into Sarah Jessica Parker's character, Carrie, in a therapist's waiting room.

Enough about them. Let's get back to my integral role. The show's four main characters find themselves in a sports bar on ladies' night. They're at a table, looking at the backs of guys sitting at the bar watching a Knicks game. That's where I come in.

No, I'm not in the bar. I'm calling the game on the TV in the bar. Kim Cattrall's character, Samantha, takes a liking to one of the gents watching the game. They eventually get together, but all this guy wants to do is watch the Knicks play on TV.

I'm Ready for My Close-Up

In another scene, Samantha and her new friend are sitting on the couch in his apartment watching the game on TV, and that's where I get to strut my stuff again, doing the play-by-play. It seems that he can only get in the mood (hey, I'm trying to keep this G-rated) when the Knicks win. In this episode, as in real life, the Knicks don't always win. To make a long story short, what I say determines whether Samantha has her way with this chap. Talk about voice command.

* * *

Another sitcom I did was a 1990s classic called *Hangin' with Mr. Cooper*, a family-oriented series that aired in prime time and was originally seen on ABC. It starred comedian Mark Curry and took place in his hometown of Oakland, California.

Curry played the lead role of Mark Cooper, a high school physical education teacher who as a younger man had failed in his bid to make the NBA. In season one, he gets a tryout with his favorite team, the Golden State Warriors.

At the time, I was the television play-by-play announcer for the Warriors, and my color commentator was former NBA player Jim Barnett. We were asked to play ourselves, calling the action in basketball scenes that involved Mr. Cooper playing in an actual NBA preseason game between the Warriors and the Phoenix Suns at the University of California, Berkeley. Both the Warriors and the Suns had agreed to this most unorthodox scenario. In fact, Warriors head coach Don Nelson and star player Tim Hardaway had acting roles along with Charles Barkley of the Suns in this two-part episode, aptly called "Warriors." The premise was that Mr. Cooper had signed a temporary contract with the Warriors and would be in uniform, wearing number 7. He was to guard Charles Barkley.

At the beginning of that live televised Warriors game, I informed the viewers that this broadcast would be different, because actor Mark Curry would be playing Mr. Cooper from his sitcom and that Jim and I would be calling him Mark Cooper on the telecast, pretending that he was a legitimate player attempting to make the team.

Granted, it was only an exhibition game but still, it was highly unusual. The sellout crowd inside Harmon Gym was tipped off to the plot, so they were really amped up.

When Don Nelson put Mr. Cooper into the game, the fans cheered loudly, and we were pumped in the broadcast booth. Sir Charles did not go easy on him. At one point, he dunked on him, then, with Coop on the ground, he looked down and said, "Welcome to the NBA." Not only that, but Mark couldn't put the ball in the ocean. However, he got a second chance.

This time, Cooper did much better and even scored a big basket down the stretch. In the end, though, he's cut from the team. It's disappointing that he doesn't make the Warriors, but there's a happy ending in that he is able to keep his job as a phys ed teacher, which he thought he had lost due to his time away for the tryout. His students even present him with a large framed Warriors jersey with the name Cooper and the number 7 to hang on the wall of the gym.

This may have been a TV first. It certainly was a first for me. You don't often call the actions of a fictional character in a real-life NBA game.

* * *

I hosted three nationally televised game shows. I was always cast as a "play-by-play" host as opposed to a traditional game show host. I couldn't shed the sportscaster typecasting.

The series that had the most longevity was *Rock N' Jock*, which debuted in 1990, the year I moved out West to call TV games for the Golden State Warriors. That's when MTV knocked on my door.

They had developed an idea for a show in which musicians, actors, and comedians played sports with professional athletes.

MTV's *Rock N' Jock Softball Challenge* and *Rock N' Jock B-Ball Jam* became pop culture sensations for about a decade. The games

I'm Ready for My Close-Up

were shot in stadiums and arenas in Southern California, and, because of the many celebrities involved, they attracted large crowds. Every event felt like a Beatles concert—many of the actors starred in the hottest shows or the biggest movies, and fans would scream at the sight of them.

The MTV producers had caught my NBA broadcasts and thought I would be the guy to call these offbeat games. They wanted a legitimate play-by-play announcer to lend authenticity. Despite that, they hired me.

These shows were a massive undertaking, but the production team, headed by Patrick Byrnes and Mitch Kozuchowski, was up to the task. Their love of sports and their ability to blend sports with show biz were key. The *Fourth Annual Rock N'Jock B-Ball Jam* was even nominated for a Daytime Emmy Award for Outstanding Game Show in 1995, only to be beaten out by *Jeopardy*.

MTV paired me with witty and clever on-air talent like Ken Ober and Chris Connelly. Another one of my color commentators was a fellow named Jon Stewart. I wonder whatever happened to him.

Seriously, working with Jon kept me on my toes. He was an MTV star at the time and an accomplished stand-up comedian who hadn't yet evolved into Jon Stewart of *The Daily Show* fame on Comedy Central. They don't come any classier.

The celebs were plentiful, including actors George Clooney, Leonardo DiCaprio, Kevin Costner, Halle Berry, Will Smith, Heather Locklear, Keanu Reeves, and Mark Wahlberg. Musicians Jon Bon Jovi, Richie Sambora, Bret Michaels, Sammy Hagar, Queen Latifah, Salt-N-Pepa, MC Hammer, Flea, and Flavor Flav joined the party. Funny people like Roseanne Barr, Tom Arnold, Michael Richards, and Sam Kinison took part.

Baseball players included Darryl Strawberry, Barry Bonds, Mark McGwire, Dwight Gooden, Ken Griffey Jr., José Canseco, Eddie Murray, and Frank Thomas. Hoopsters included Magic Johnson, Reggie Miller, Vlade Divac, Gary Payton, and Shawn Kemp. Kareem Abdul Jabbar, Shaquille O'Neal, and Bill Walton served as coaches.

The powerhouse combination of athletes and entertainers playing sports together created entertainment gold.

The rules for the basketball games were groundbreaking. The three-point shot? Forget it. *Rock N' Jock* introduced the twenty-five-point basket and, yes, the fifty-point shot.

The antics for the softball games were brilliant. Mets relief pitcher Roger McDowell set the tone when he first walked in from the bullpen wearing a bra on the outside of his uniform. The games even included farm animals roaming in the outfield.

It was always fun and games announcing for MTV *Rock N' Jock* as I'm attempting to interview Darryl Strawberry (left).

I never knew what to expect. During a postgame interview with Darryl Strawberry, players and celebrities were stuffing water bottles, dirt, and grass down my back. I never flinched. It was exactly what the showrunners wanted, and I was happy to play along. But afterward, I did have a hefty dry-cleaning bill for MTV.

I'm Ready for My Close-Up

Celebrities flocked to *Rock N' Jock*, like movie star Kevin Costner (left), who took the time to talk to me on the air.

* * *

The Grudge Match was a sports competition game show that was taped in front of an audience at Universal Studios in Universal City, California. Airing in syndication in 1991, the show pitted feuding folks against one another in a boxing ring to settle their grievances. They would seek revenge using various objects, such as oversized boxing gloves, batakas, or clubs. Food items, including stale donuts, a complete salad bar, or a full Las Vegas buffet, were offered as weapons. Chocolate pudding, cakes, and pies also found their way into the arsenal.

I did the blow-by-blow, or in some cases the spaghetti-by-spaghetti, of this messy mayhem, and my broadcast partner was wrestler-turned-actor-turned-politician Jesse "The Body" Ventura.

A Funny Thing Happened on the Way to the Broadcast Booth

Prior to each match, famed ring announcer Michael Buffer would introduce the contestants, just as he would for a professional prizefight. The referee was stand-up comedian John Pinette, who appeared in the final episode of Seinfeld. After the combatants beat the stuffing out of each other, often with actual Thanksgiving stuffing, Jesse would hop into the ring to do post-fight interviews.

The show's creator, Rich Melcombe, who was in the process of developing *The Grudge Match,* happened to be in the Showtime production truck one day, visiting boxing director Bob Dunphy (son of my blow-by-blow idol Don Dunphy) while we were rehearsing an outdoor telecast in Las Vegas. As dusk fell and the temperature dropped, to entertain my ringside partners, I was being goofy and broke into my Jerry Lewis impersonation. Rich hired me.

I went from a legitimate boxing ring to *The Grudge Match* ring, where contestants fought over issues that would usually pop up in small claims court or on *The People's Court* with Judge Wapner. In one dispute, for example, a guy wrote his term paper on a computer only to have it erased by his girlfriend, and he wanted payback. Another grudge match centered around a woman who lent her wedding gown to a friend, who turned it into a miniskirt.

Once, former Los Angeles Dodger standout Steve Garvey was in the ring, fighting his agent. That was one bout I could relate to. Another time, former boxing champion Thomas "Hit Man" Hearns joined Jesse and me to describe the action. Hearns ate it up, and I don't mean the food that came flying through the ropes.

The Grudge Match caught the eye of the producers of *The Phil Donahue Show*, and the entire cast, including me, were guests on the popular NBC daytime program. Phil seemed genuinely engaged with this off-the-wall premise, and the studio audience had fun with it as well.

Behind the scenes, the production and talent coordinators were Melissa Rivers and Lyla Michaels. Melissa's mother was comic legend Joan Rivers, and Lyla was the mother of renowned sportscaster Al Michaels. Joan once visited the set, but Al never

I'm Ready for My Close-Up

made the scene. Too bad. A grudge match between Joan and Al would have made for a ratings bonanza.

Coming from the world of traditional sports, this was clearly an out-of-the-box experience for me. Still, I approached each match like the real thing . . . but with tongue firmly in cheek.

With my *Grudge Match* broadcast partner, future governor of Minnesota Jesse Ventura (right).

* * *

From 1999 to 2001, I hosted a nationally syndicated show called *Battle Dome. Battle Dome* was part sports competition game show, part reality TV, and totally intense.

The pilot was shot on the *Wheel of Fortune* set at Sony Pictures Studios in Culver City, California, while the cast and crew of that iconic show was on hiatus. Believe it or not, I was assigned Vanna

A Funny Thing Happened on the Way to the Broadcast Booth

White's dressing room. The only catch? To unlock the door, I had to buy a vowel.

Once *Battle Dome* was greenlit, the production moved to the Los Angeles Memorial Sports Arena. My first booth partner was outspoken sports talk show personality Scott Ferrall, who was followed by Ed Lover, co-host of the popular MTV series *Yo! MTV Raps*.

Battle Dome pitted "warriors" against "challengers." The "warriors" made theatrical entrances, then competed against the "challengers" in physically grueling events like the Battle Wheel, Aerial Kickboxing, and the Rollercage of Fire. It was not for the faint of heart. A couple of competitors suffered ugly injuries. It was the first time I did play-by-play with a hand over one eye. Well, maybe the second time. Remember, I announced for the Mets in the late '70s and early '80s.

The biggest celebrity to emerge from this spectacle was Terry Crews. He played the warrior known as T-Money. A former defensive end and linebacker in the NFL, Terry's character was a smug, arrogant guy who was always accompanied by his posse. He wore a lot of bling and sported a dollar sign necklace. T-Money did not like to lose.

In real life, Terry was nothing like T-Money. He exuded humility. He was a natural in front of the camera, and performing on the *Battle Dome* stage lit a fire in him for a career in acting. He went on to become a star of the big and small screens.

With his engaging personality, you couldn't help but root for Terry. I'm glad he survived his demanding *Battle Dome* experience.

Me? I managed to survive the game show genre in the broadcast booth and at ringside. I wanted to challenge myself with these unconventional projects. Perhaps I craved more than mainstream sports, or maybe I was simply curious.

Eventually, I got back to basics, but I continued to dip my toe into uncharted waters. It made life interesting.

Tastes Great. Less Filling!

One of the best career moves I ever made was getting my SAG card. It gave me the chance to do much more than I had imagined when I got into broadcasting.

SAG stands for Screen Actors Guild, a labor union that represents film and television principal and background performers throughout the world. In 2012, SAG merged with the American Federation of Television and Radio Artists (AFTRA) to become SAG-AFTRA.

I got my SAG card in 1972, after graduating from Kent State. Somebody said, "Get your SAG card so you can do commercials." I'm guessing it was a talent agent. It was a great move, as voice-overs and commercials played an integral role in my career.

I voiced countless television and radio commercials through the years, for almost any product you can imagine. That included a

A Funny Thing Happened on the Way to the Broadcast Booth

Tostitos TV ad that aired during a Super Bowl. That's about as good as it gets.

Another dandy was a television spot for Domino's. In the ad, I shouted that your pizza would be free if it wasn't delivered in a half hour. Soon after, I had some friends over to watch the NHL All-Star Game, and we ordered a Domino's pizza. A snowstorm had walloped New York City that day, and we waited over an hour for the delivery person to arrive. When he came to the door, my commercial was on the TV, and you could hear me hollering, "Your Domino's pizza is free if it's not delivered in a half hour!" The delivery man handed me the large pizza box and said that since he hadn't gotten there in a half hour, it was on the house. I looked out the window and saw the brutal weather conditions. I felt so bad for the guy, I not only paid him the full price of the pizza but gave him a generous tip.

Whenever a frenetic, high-energy play-by-play announcer was needed to yell "*unbelievable!*" I usually received a phone call from my agency to audition. I didn't always win the audition, but I got my share of bookings.

One of the funnier voice-overs was for a cleaning product, when I did play-by-play of two mops racing around a house. They wanted a straight call, as if it were two runners sprinting to the finish line.

Speaking of sprinting, I invested in a pair of comfortable shoes. There's an old expression, "Hey kid, you're going places." That could mean auditioning, because I was going downtown, midtown, uptown, all around the town.

Then there was the mental aspect of auditioning. I could do an audition and think I nailed it. Of course, I wouldn't hear back. Then, I could audition and think, "No way, it just didn't feel right." The next day, I would get the booking.

At times, I would have to compete with professional voice-over actors, who were often hired to play the roles of sportscasters or play-by-play announcers. Casting agents are looking for that certain sound, and, in my opinion, they don't know what it is until they hear it. Sometimes this means they choose an actor over a real-life play-by-play announcer.

I learned never to take audition outcomes personally. I had so many slaps in the face that if I had taken each one to heart, I would be standing on the edge of the Brooklyn Bridge with someone trying to talk me down.

The auditions were cattle calls—sportscasters, play-by-play announcers, actors, voice-over artists—all packed into a small room like a herd of cattle. Many would pace up and down, reading the script aloud.

Today you can avoid the cattle calls. Many voice-over artists install recording equipment in their homes or use a mobile app. You can audition in your pajamas. But even with these technological advances, sometimes they still require you to go to a studio. For that, I don't recommend pajamas.

When I entered the studio, I gave it my best shot. One time, I was auditioning for a commercial and the casting director said to me, "We're looking for a Marv Albert type." This person obviously didn't realize that I was Marv's brother or simply overlooked my last name. When he cued me, I did my best Marv impersonation. You guessed it—I didn't get the job. I have a feeling if Marv himself had auditioned, he wouldn't have gotten it either.

Ironically, the biggest commercial I ever landed did not require an audition. This was more than a voice-over. It was a series of three or four television commercials in which I would be on camera, joining the fraternity of the celebrated long-running Miller Lite "Tastes Great. Less Filling" campaign.

Miller Lite commercials debuted in 1975. The ads featured famous pop culture personalities like Rodney Dangerfield, Mickey Spillane, Bob Uecker, Bubba Smith, Billy Martin, and George Steinbrenner. The campaign is considered one of the best in advertising history.

It was now 1989, and I had hit the jackpot. I was to play the role of a football announcer in spots shot in Los Angeles that would star actor George Wendt, who played Norm on *Cheers*, and Richard Moll, who portrayed Bull on *Night Court*, two popular shows at the time. The ads also featured NFL royalty who were already members of the Miller Lite club, like Dolphins great Larry Csonka, Jets star Joe Klecko, Raiders legends Otis Sistrunk and Ben Davidson, 49ers hero Dwight Clark, Colts sensation Bert Jones, and then some.

To direct the commercial, they had brought in the accomplished Howard Zieff, who directed such movies as *Private Benjamin*, *Hearts of the West*, and *The Dream Team*. His best-known commercials were the Alka-Seltzer "Mamma Mia, that's a spicy meatball" spot and ads for Levy's real Jewish Rye Bread that had the memorable tag line "You don't have to be Jewish to love Levy's." He cast some unknown young actors by the names of Robert De Niro, Dustin Hoffman, and Richard Dreyfuss in commercials.

One morning, the entire Miller Lite cast was standing in the hotel lobby, waiting for the bus to take us to a football field to shoot. Suddenly, in walked James Garner, star of epic movies like *The Great Escape* and *Grand Prix* and TV blockbusters like *Maverick* and *The Rockford Files*.

We all formed a line from the hotel entrance across to the front desk, and James Garner, with a big smile, stopped in front of each person to shake his hand. It looked like a receiving line for Queen Elizabeth, but don't worry, I didn't curtsy when he got to me. I don't know who was more excited, James or the rest of us. This was long before phone cameras, maybe a good thing for Mr. Garner, or he would have had to take a selfie with each and every one of us. I think he might have enjoyed it. Too bad we didn't have a refreshing six-pack of Miller Lite for him as a parting gift.

Then there was the time I was shooting a scene with George Wendt on a football field. George played the role of the star player in the commercial, Wild Willy Wendt. In this scene, I had to interview him. George and I were kneeling on the ground directly in front of each other, almost nose to nose. The camera was right next to us, and Howard Zieff was standing alongside the camera. Howard said to us, "Okay, anytime you're ready."

I was holding a microphone and staring straight at George. This went on for a few seconds, then a few more seconds, and yes, a few more seconds. I was waiting for George to say his line, and I was to respond. The problem was, I had forgotten that I had the first line, and George was being polite. Maybe he figured I was method acting or something and getting myself all motivated before speaking. We basically just stared at other for what seemed like forever.

George finally said in hushed tones, "Uh, Steve, I think you're supposed to go first."

Man, did my face turn red. George just smiled and said, "No worries, it happens to the best of them." Thankfully, we got the shot on the next take, and we were able to move on.

The final scene of the last commercial was shot in a locker room set on a soundstage in LA. There I was, in my neatly pressed blue blazer, shirt, and tie, with my trusty hand mic prop, interviewing the winning coach, played by Richard Moll, and closely surrounded by all the players. We were instructed to get really close to one another.

In the scene, Richard was to throw some Super Bowl tickets in the air, and the players were to dive after them on the floor. We had to do the scene several times, and this is where I really earned my money. The former NFL players were large, muscular human beings, and each time they dove on the floor, it was my skinny bones that wound up at the bottom of the heap. After I was crushed in each take, we all had to get up and do it again . . . and again. I felt like Wile E. Coyote after being flattened in an unsuccessful catapult launch.

After that bruising final scene, I hobbled gingerly to the bus for the ride back to the hotel. It was a good feeling knowing we had done the job well and that another series of Miller Lite commercials was in the can. I was just happy I wasn't in traction.

A Funny Thing Happened on the Way to the Broadcast Booth

Just When You Thought I Had Done It All

He's done it, he's done it! Robbie Knievel has done it and they're going crazy! They're going crazy at Caesars Palace! Robbie Knievel, the first person to successfully jump the fountains of Caesars Palace, avenging his father, the legendary Evel Knievel!"

That's my play-by-play call of a motorcycle jump on April 14, 1989, in Las Vegas, Nevada. If somebody had told me when I first got into broadcasting that I would be doing some of the things I did, I wouldn't have believed it.

You've heard of Evel Knievel, the daredevil? His son Robbie, an accomplished motorcyclist and stunt performer himself, decided it was his turn to attempt a jump that nearly cost Evel his life.

A Funny Thing Happened on the Way to the Broadcast Booth

When Evel tried the stunt in 1967, he hit the takeoff ramp and tumbled over his motorcycle handlebars onto the pavement, then skidded into the parking lot of the Dunes Hotel. It left him with a crushed pelvis and femur, fractures to his hip, wrist, and both ankles, and a concussion. There were rumors that he was in a coma for twenty-nine days. After that jump attempt, Evel's brand was bigger than ever.

Evel's career was a tough act to follow. Robbie, however, wanted to pay homage to his father by flying over the fountains of Caesars Palace on his bike. The one thing about his dad that he did not want to emulate was his record for most bones broken in a lifetime, a record that is immortalized in *Guinness World Records*.

I was hired to do the play-by-play for the nationally syndicated cable television broadcast. I was sitting alone in an elevated broadcast booth that had been constructed solely for this spectacle. It was located on the front edge of the hotel property, bordering the bustling Las Vegas Strip. Color commentators Dave Diles and Dave Despain reported from ground level.

The city had closed off a large portion of the Strip to vehicular traffic near Caesars but allowed pedestrians to gather in the closed area. The crowd was enormous. From my lofty perch, I could see curiosity seekers for miles.

The night before the broadcast at around eleven o'clock, the phone in my room rang.

I picked it up and said, "Hello?"

In a sharp, raspy voice, the caller said, "Steve?"

"Yes."

Evel Knievel was calling me to ask who was going to interview him during the broadcast. He said, "I don't want anyone interviewing me but you."

I said, "I appreciate that Evel, but, unfortunately, that's not my decision. The producer decides that."

He replied, "If anybody else does the interview, I'm going to give only one-word answers."

Just When You Thought I Had Done It All

I said, "Evel, I don't think you'll really do that."

He said, "Okay, goodnight."

In the days leading up to Robbie's jump, I had gotten to bond with Evel. We both had hockey backgrounds, mine as an announcer, his as a player. Beyond his eccentricities, he was a good egg. Perhaps he felt more comfortable with me. In any event, he did his interview the next day with one of my broadcast partners, and it was great. Whether he was riding a motorcycle or just talking, Evel was always entertaining.

On the live broadcast, I was to serve as the host and point man up in the booth, but this sort of play-by-play was unfamiliar to me.

I had never announced a death-defying event in which I had to be ready for three possible scenarios. The first was that Robbie would clear the fountains without a scratch. The second? That he would crash but survive, which was the case when his father had attempted the same jump. The third scenario? I didn't even want to think about it. I prayed that I wouldn't have to say those words.

The anticipation was building as Robbie made several practice run-ups to the ramp. He had never made this long a jump. It was a distance of 170 feet. Every time he motored up that ramp, my heart skipped a beat. Was this the moment he would really take off, or would he race up that ramp and then stop? Only Robbie knew when the time was right. It was nerve-racking.

The practice approaches went on for quite a while. Each time Robbie revved his bike and started to accelerate, the massive crowd roared. He looked like a superhero, dressed in his fancy white jumpsuit trimmed in blue and red. As he circled around again and got into position, we heard the "vroom vroom" of his cycle. Then he made his fifth and what turned out to be final approach to the incline. I could sense that this time it was for real.

He sped up the ramp and soared into the air like a jet off an elevated runway. Then he sailed majestically over the fountains. The bike's wheels glided safely down onto the pavement at the other end, and the crowd exploded in cheers.

A Funny Thing Happened on the Way to the Broadcast Booth

Thank goodness, I was able to use the first scenario. After the epic jump, Robbie said, "That was for you, Dad," and father and son embraced. I was never in my life more relieved after calling an event.

* * *

If you thought that was out of my wheelhouse, here's another doozy. It's called *Elmo's Potty Time.*

When the kind folks at *Sesame Street* requested my services, I knew I had arrived. Either that, or my career was going down the toilet (Ba Dum Bum).

It wasn't my first foray into educational television. Earlier in my career, I did a segment for the long-running PBS children's series *Reading Rainbow*, starring Levar Burton. I portrayed myself on camera as the play-by-play announcer for a girls' baseball game. It was filmed in my old stomping grounds of Brooklyn, New York, in 1989 and was part of an episode entitled "Dinosaur Bob and His Adventures with the Family Lazardo," based on a children's book of the same title. I called the action and did postgame interviews with the kids, as if it were a real big-league game.

As delightful as that was, it would be difficult to top my experience participating in the timeless video known as *Elmo's Potty Time* in 2005. In one of the segments, I did the play-by-play description of a little girl who was demonstrating the correct way to wash her hands in the bathroom.

For years after I did that video, parents were coming up to thank me for helping their young children learn how to wash their hands in the bathroom. As atypical as it was, it was one of the most rewarding things I had ever done as a broadcaster.

You never know where this business will lead you and, as I discovered, you have to be ready for anything. In the next chapter, "My First Broadcast Booth," I describe how as a kid, I announced ping-pong, family dinners, and hamster Olympics at home. It was perfect training, and I knew it would pay off someday.

Just When You Thought I Had Done It All

* * *

Many of us have played dodgeball. Announcing it is another story. Not only was I brought in to call this lightning-fast action, but I was to call it while sitting between Ben Stiller and Vince Vaughn.

It was an MTV production to promote the actors' comedy film, *Dodgeball: A True Underdog Story*. By the time the movie hit theaters in 2004, I was an MTV veteran, having called many years of *Rock N' Jock* events. The cable channel kept it in the family and brought me in to do the play-by-play.

If you think it might be intimidating to sit between Ben Stiller and Vince Vaughn, you're right. Try matching wits with them.

The three of us were called upon to announce a series of dodgeball games at a gym in Santa Monica, California. I was to do the play-by-play while the two stars provided color commentary. I had been given a list of players' names and numbers prior to the shoot, but once the games started, the action was so fast and furious it was almost impossible to slip them in. There was no time at all to include any biographical background information on these people. The games were a blur.

Much of my play-by-play consisted of astute comments like, "Ooh," "oh," "wow," "ouch," "look out," "yikes," "that had to hurt," and "that'll leave a mark!"

Most of the analysis by Ben and Vince was pretty similar to my spot-on play-by-play. This stream of narrative brilliance went on for a while, with no letup in the action. It was impossible to inject any witty repartee. At one point, I said to myself that it was time to change things up.

During a rare break in the action, I thought I would admire Ben's silky-soft velour shirt. I must have struck a chord in the production truck, because the producer told me to keep doing that.

I said, "Ben, I really like your shirt.

Ben replied, "Oh, well, thank you, Steve."

"No really, Ben, I love that shirt."

"Thanks again, Steve."

Then I asked him where he got the shirt and how much he paid for it. I could sense now that Ben was getting a little irritated by this bizarre line of questioning. The producer then said in my ear, "Keep it going, Steve. Ben gets funnier when he starts to get annoyed."

In the meantime, Vince, sitting next to me, was losing it, trying to keep from laughing out loud. He too knew how this would affect Ben. Vince gave me a thumbs up to indicate that I was going in the right direction.

Then I said, "Hey, Ben?"

Ben, more irritated, replied, "Yes, Steve."

I blurted out, "Can I have your shirt, when you're done with it?"

Ben said, "What, you want my shirt? You know something, Steve?"

"What's that, Ben?"

"You used to be my favorite Albert brother!" he exclaimed.

I heard in my ear from the producer, "Bingo! That's what we were going for."

Vince was all smiles. He was loving it, and that was a sweet feeling. I was able to get Ben Stiller to deliver a funny line, and I got Vince Vaughn to crack up. It doesn't get much better than that.

* * *

When I worked at WWWE radio in Cleveland, calling the Crusaders hockey games, the station was looking for other assignments to fill out my schedule during the off-season. Aside from having me anchor morning sports reports, they asked me if I would be interested in doing play-by-play for the Cleveland Nets of World Team Tennis.

I asked, "On the radio?"

"Yes."

In case I hadn't heard them correctly, I repeated, "Let me get this straight, you want me to announce tennis . . . on the radio? Seriously? Okay, I'll give it a shot."

Just When You Thought I Had Done It All

I had never called a tennis match before, and I associated the sport with television only. Whoever heard of tennis on the radio? I later learned that tennis matches were carried on BBC radio in England. I may have been the first to call tennis on the radio in the United States. After my performance, I was probably the last.

Playing tennis is one thing, announcing it is another. I needed to bone up on the rules and intricacies of the sport, so I went out and bought every book I could find on it.

Then I made a list of descriptive tennis terms, just as I did for hockey. Like other sports, tennis had its vernacular. For example, "there's a beautiful crosscourt volley for the winner," "a gorgeous passing shot down the line," and "a perfect lob that lands just inside the baseline."

I couldn't just flick on the radio and catch the play-by-play of a tennis match for research purposes. In addition, the rules and regulations of World Team Tennis were different from standard tournament competition. One controversial aspect of the league was that crowd members were not only allowed to cheer during play, they were encouraged to do so. The players didn't exactly jump for joy over this. The organizers wanted to generate fan participation, which was a plus from my standpoint because it allowed me to deliver the play-by-play in my normal voice or even enthusiastically. I didn't have to speak in a whisper.

The Nets played their home matches in a venerable building called Public Hall in downtown Cleveland. It was an intimate venue with a balcony overhang, so the fans were practically breathing down the players' necks. When the crowd noise started, particularly before a serve, you could see the players cringing, but this is what they'd signed up for and they had to deal with it.

World Team Tennis was an intriguing concept that was launched in 1973 by Dennis Murphy, who had started the World Hockey Association. WTT began play in 1974 with sixteen teams. Besides the Cleveland Nets, there were the New York Sets, Denver Racquets, Detroit Loves, Los Angeles Strings, and, well, you get the idea.

The league had some big names, starting with Billie Jean King, one of the greatest tennis players of all time. Tennis legends Jimmy Connors and Chris Evert were also onboard. Elton John, a friend of Billie Jean's, wrote a theme song for the Philly team, known as the Freedoms, a little ditty called "Philadelphia Freedom."

Announcing World Team Tennis home and away kept me busy in the summer. I may be the only person who's announced for two teams named the Nets in two different sports. Not long after I called games for the Cleveland Nets, I did play-by-play for the New York Nets basketball team, and later, when they moved to New Jersey.

For the tennis Nets, I had to flap my mouth pretty fast, maybe even faster than for hockey. Tennis is not exactly tailored for radio, and it was challenging.

The local ABC affiliate also hired me to call selected matches on TV. The cool thing about that was that my color commentators were sports royalty. I was paired with the aforementioned Billie Jean King and former Cleveland Indians owner Bill Veeck, a popular figure at the time in Northeast Ohio.

With thirty-nine Grand Slam titles and formerly the number one tennis player in the world, Billie Jean knew a thing or two about the sport. She had beaten Bobby Riggs in the Battle of the Sexes mega match and gotten Virginia Slims to sponsor women's tennis.

How many announcers can say their broadcast partner was responsible for the exploding scoreboard? Bill Veeck was one of baseball's master innovators, creator of fireworks nights and giveaway promotions like Bat Day.

While tennis on radio started out as a foreign concept to me, it was a blessing in disguise. I learned that if you can do tennis on radio, you can probably do anything.

My First Broadcast Booth

It was 1958. Eisenhower was president, Hula-Hoops were a national craze, a gallon of gas cost a quarter, and there was only one baseball team in New York. I'm pretty sure I was the youngest sportscaster on my block. The second- and third-youngest were my two older brothers.

In a corner room on the first floor of our house, we created a little world where we got to announce sports. It was our make-believe sportscasting school, where we were the students as well as the teachers. I can remember vividly the day when I called my first play-by-play.

In my squeaky voice, I yelled, "Here's the pitch!"

My brother Marv made a cracking sound with two large pencils.

A Funny Thing Happened on the Way to the Broadcast Booth

I continued even more excitedly, "There's a long drive to deep left field. That ball is . . . gone! Mickey Mantle has just driven one into the seats in left as the fans chase after that souvenir!"

My other brother Al cranked up the sound of the crowd, which we had on a record of sound effects.

At this point, my voice rose to a full shout. "And the crowd is going wild! They're all standing here at Yankee Stadium as the Mick does it again! It's another home run for number seven, Mickey Mantle! And the Yankees take the lead, two to one!"

The phonograph needle screeched to a halt and the crowd noise stopped. Suddenly, the room was silent. I looked at both of my brothers and asked, "How was that?"

Marv responded, "Not bad, Steve. That sounded pretty good. Maybe next time, bring the excitement level down just a little."

"Thanks," I replied.

Then seventeen-year-old Marv said, "Okay, let's switch around now. I'll control the crowd noise. Steve, you handle the sound of the bat. Al, you do the play-by-play."

"That's swell," said Al. I smiled, nodding in agreement.

* * *

For me, it all began in that little room in Manhattan Beach, Brooklyn. We set up a makeshift press box with our parents' folding card table, three rickety chairs, and a small black and white TV. Our broadcasting equipment consisted of a Revere reel-to-reel tape recorder, a sound effects record, and two grease pencils. The only thing missing was an "on the air" sign.

The Little Room, as it was affectionately known to my brothers and me, became my first broadcast booth, and a place where dreams were born. It's a safe bet that ours was the only house in the neighborhood that had one. Not bad for an eight-year-old kid who fantasized about someday becoming a sports announcer.

My First Broadcast Booth

As a shy little boy, the only time I had any confidence was in that cramped room, announcing alongside my two older brothers. It was like a cocoon, a reprieve from things like being called on by my teacher to answer a question in front of the entire class or, worse yet, talk to a girl.

So now Al, who was twelve, slid over to the chair on the right, next to the tape recorder and microphone, Marv sat in the middle behind the record player, and I took the seat on the left for my next assignment.

We would turn on the Yankees game on WPIX Channel 11. Sometimes the picture was fuzzy, so we'd have to adjust the rabbit ears. Then we would turn down the sound of the real announcers, Mel Allen and the Ol' Redhead, Red Barber. No offense—they were great, but this was our little world, and we were in charge. Besides, we didn't want Mel and Red to drown us out.

We used the monstrously large tape recorder to record our play-by-play.

Marv would lug that contraption around Ebbets Field when he worked as an office boy for the Brooklyn Dodgers. During games, he would drag the bulky machine up into the stands, sit next to the fans, and practice his play-by-play. The fans started to complain about this kid announcing next to them as they tried to enjoy the game. Word got back to team owner Walter O'Malley, who made Marv stop.

Here in the Little Room, we didn't have to deal with unappreciative fans.

That tape recorder was a valuable asset. It allowed us to play back and listen, to improve.

We used an LP sound effects record on our phonograph, which sat on our press box table. When we lowered the sound of the real Yankees announcers on the TV, we also lost the sound of the crowd. We had to manufacture our own crowd noise.

The sound effects record had a wide variety of noises on it, ranging from city traffic and jungle sounds to laughter and applause.

A Funny Thing Happened on the Way to the Broadcast Booth

The sound that mattered most to us was that of a baseball crowd. The problem was it lasted for only about two minutes. You had to be catlike quick to put the needle back to the beginning of the baseball crowd, to keep the noise going. It wasn't easy to find the exact groove on the vinyl disc. Sometimes, we would put it too far back and suddenly, in the middle of a three and two pitch to Moose Skowron with the bases loaded, we would hear cars crashing into each other, dogs barking, or some other sound effect.

Then there was the sound of the bat hitting the ball. To recreate that, we got a big assist from our father. He would bring home from his grocery store these big grease pencils used to mark prices on products. We figured out that when you knocked the pencils together hard, it simulated the crack of a bat. I would closely monitor the action on the TV, and at the appropriate moments, I would slam the two pencils together to create the "thwack" of the bat.

When we combined these elements, it sounded just like we were at the ballpark. Well, not exactly, but it was close enough for our purposes.

In the end, we all got an opportunity to get real play-by-play experience, from the comfort of our own home. While some people might have thought, had they stumbled into that room, that we should be committed, we thought what we were doing was perfectly normal . . . for three kids obsessed with becoming sportscasters.

We weren't a hundred percent sure where all of this was heading, and, believe me, my parents had no idea what was going on behind that closed door. One thing I do know: They never told us to stop, and for that, I am eternally grateful.

After making my play-by-play debut in the Little Room, it was time to move up in grade by going down to the basement.

We lived on Kensington Street, so we dubbed our basement Kensington Square Garden, an homage to Madison Square Garden. If our basement had a big showy marquee like the Garden, it would have proclaimed "PING-PONG TONIGHT" in neon lights. That was our sport of choice in the basement. Oops, make that, in Kensington Square Garden.

From time to time, my parents used the basement for dance parties with their friends and neighbors. But mostly, we commandeered it, leaving no trace of their mambo gatherings. Ping-pong became our fixation, but these were not just ordinary ho-hum ping-pong matches. It was ping-pong with a soundtrack of loud, boisterous play-by-play.

My brothers and I (from left, Marv, Al, and me) in our Brooklyn home taking a timeout from our homemade broadcasting "school." I think I still have that outfit.

Like clockwork, every night after dinner, my brothers and I would race thunderously down the long stairway into the dark recesses of the basement. We would flick on the lights and there it was, an olive-colored ping-pong table that seemed to glitter like gold. It took up nearly the entire room, so there wasn't much space for maneuvering. Did I say it glittered like gold? It was more grizzled than glittering, and battered with many, many deep scratches on the edges, the results of banging our paddles on the table in disgust after missing shots.

Two of us would engage in mortal combat at the table while the third would announce, calling the action, complete with commercials during breaks. We had actual professional advertising copy that Marv brought home from one of his early radio jobs. The games were the focal point of our evening activities, and when I say it was mortal combat, I'm not exaggerating much. It got to the point where ping-pong paddles were soaring across the table like pies in a Three Stooges short. I mean, it got nasty. Al led the league in throwing his paddle, which gave Marv and me endless opportunities to practice our ducking skills.

Imagine Marv calling the play-by-play while Al and I smacked the ball back and forth: "Steve swats a line drive over the net. Al returns it with a beautiful backhand. Now Steve lofts one high and Al delivers a crushing blast for the winner. What a shot!"

Upstairs in the quieter quarters of the house, my mother would hear the clamor coming from the basement and scream at the top of her lungs, "What's going on down there?"

It was like a scene out of the movie *The King of Comedy*, with Robert De Niro. Remember his character, Rupert Pupkin? He's a wannabe comedian who makes believe he hosts a late-night talk show in the basement of his house, complete with life-size cardboard cutouts of his celebrity guests. His mother would yell, "Rupert, what are you doing down there? You're gonna be late for work." My mother's annoyance with our basement antics happened way before *The King of Comedy* came out, but you could make an argument that we were the Rupert Pupkins of sportscasting.

My First Broadcast Booth

My poor mother must have thought we had gone off the deep end, probably wondering, "Who does this sort of thing?" It may have seemed strange at the time, but we had a feeling it was for a reason and that someday it would all make sense. None of it made much sense to my mother at the time. We drove her bananas.

My mother Alida (right), brother Al (left), and I (center) yukking it up for the camera in our Brooklyn backyard.

Combat ping-pong was just the tip of the iceberg. Al and I used to horse around upstairs in the house. We were both into professional wrestling. We knew it was fake, but we still liked it. Haystack Calhoun, Baby Huey, and Killer Kowalski were our favorite wrestlers. Haystack and Baby were humongous. They had to be at least four hundred pounds each. Calhoun had a scruffy beard and wore overalls. Huey wore a diaper. Kowalski looked like an old-movie version of an escapee from an institution for the criminally insane. His famous claw hold put opponents to sleep.

A Funny Thing Happened on the Way to the Broadcast Booth

The two of us would stuff pillows under our shirts and imitate these larger-than-life characters. We would jump up and down on our beds, drop onto our stomachs with the pillows cushioning the impact, then bounce back up. Naturally, while this hubbub was going on, we were announcing it. Miraculously, our beds didn't collapse, but it sounded like they were going to crash through the floor into the kitchen below, where my mother was cooking dinner.

"What are you boys doing up there?" she would holler from downstairs, sounding very much like Edith Bunker, years before *All in the Family*. "You're gonna break down the house," she'd yell sometimes and, when she was really frustrated, she would declare, "Wait 'til your father comes home!" Bingo. That was the clincher.

Then we would hear the clunking footsteps. My mother would come busting up the stairway like Jim Brown. Instead of a football, she wielded a large, thick wooden spoon.

When Mom ran toward us brandishing the ominous-looking weapon, we would bob and weave, head fake, sidestep, and run like deer to evade her. Whizzing past her like the Road Runner, we'd dash down the stairs and out the front door into the street. Thank goodness we could outrun our mother. Otherwise, I shudder to think of the consequences. It's a little late to apologize, but sorry mom.

* * *

I couldn't wait until Marv went off to college. Nothing personal, I just wanted his room. While the Little Room and the basement were instrumental in our play-by-play development, Marv's room, although the size of a shoebox, was like a built-in broadcast booth.

Marv's room had a large window that faced the street. I could sit there all day and announce stickball, punchball, stoopball, and hit the penny, the classic Brooklyn street games. Better yet, it was like being behind home plate at Fenway Park or Tiger Stadium, where the booths were close to the field. The overhang of the house put me right above the street action. When my father bought our house in

My First Broadcast Booth

1950, I don't think he figured on certain rooms serving as broadcast booths for his future sportscaster sons. He was pretty smart, but psychic? That might be a stretch.

We would parade around the house and announce almost anything. We even did play-by-play of dinner. Here's a sample:

> It all comes down to this. There's dad at the head of the table. He grabs his fork. What's he gonna do? He takes a stab at the brisket and jams it into his mouth. Oh, that'll leave a mark! Okay, here comes mom with the mashed potatoes and gravy. Look out, she spills the gravy! That's not what she had in mind. And the big *E* for "error" lights up on the scoreboard! Wait a second, here comes a substitution. It's grandpa off the couch! And he is . . . *hungry*! Now, a word from our sponsor.

Perhaps the kookiest thing I ever did in terms of play-by-play calls in the house was when I staged a sports extravaganza called the Hamster Olympics. I had two hamsters at different times. The first one was named Ambrose. After Ambrose went up to the great hamster wheel in the sky, I adopted Zachary. My friend Kenny would bring his hamster over to the house, and the two rodents would compete in various events. We had the traditional hamster wheel competition to see which hamster could last longer before tiring out. We used the couch, which was encased in plastic, for long jump events.

My mother, incidentally, put plastic covers on just about anything that didn't move. That's probably why my brothers and I all stayed so active. It was a means of survival.

We also had a contest to see which hamster could stuff more food into his cheek pouches. Of course, I would do the play-by-play for these epic games. I figured at the time that if ABC ever decided to

A Funny Thing Happened on the Way to the Broadcast Booth

add a Hamster Olympics to its *Wide World of Sports* coverage, forget Jim McKay. I was their man.

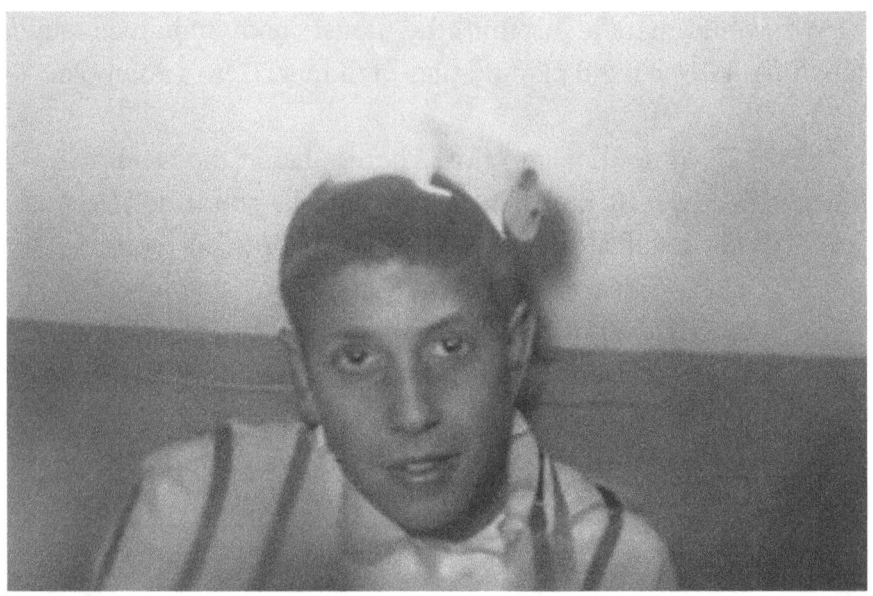

That's Ambrose getting a "head" start for the Hamster Olympics when I was thirteen.

To me, this all felt normal. Sure, I think I realized, even at that age, that what we were doing might have been perceived as somewhat abnormal behavior. There probably weren't too many other kids going around the house and announcing almost everything that took place.

My parents perhaps thought we were simply going through a phase. My mother was probably thinking—make that praying—that the next "phase" would involve a stethoscope instead of a microphone.

* * *

I grew up in a Brooklyn middle-class neighborhood that was predominantly Jewish.

Being of the faith, my mother kept a kosher household, which meant we didn't mix meat with dairy. I remember the first time I came home from college and melted a piece of American cheese on top of a hamburger. My mom almost had a heart attack.

We weren't ultrareligious, but I could see the joy on my mother's face during my bar mitzvah. Contrary to popular belief, I did not read my haftorah off a teleprompter. I did raise a few eyebrows, though, when I said, "We'll be back with the rabbi's sermon right after these messages."

Before I came into this world, my parents lived in the neighboring community of Brighton Beach, which consisted mainly of storefronts and apartments. They lived in a building under the El, the elevated train. My mother told me that every few minutes, the train would rumble by like a hurricane, seemingly inches from my parents' windows. The noise was deafening and it felt almost like an earthquake, she said, literally rearranging the furniture. My mother might be knitting in a chair in the living room, and the next thing she knew, she was sitting next to the kitchen sink. I can't imagine living like that. They said they got used to it.

I was fortunate that they moved to the quiet residential community of Manhattan Beach when I was born, an ideal place to grow up, particularly for three aspiring sportscasters.

We got to watch some of the best basketball players on earth at Manhattan Beach Park, right in our own backyard. The great ones, like playground legends Connie Hawkins, Billy Cunningham, Roger Brown, and Art Heyman, always played on basket number one, just inside the fence. The sun-drenched locals were ten deep around the court.

We had the P.S. 195 schoolyard, which featured our own form of the Green Monster, the fabled wall at Fenway Park in Boston. It was a short softball poke, but the fence was high. On weekends, the gates were locked, so we had to climb the fence to get in. It was risky, but worth it.

A Funny Thing Happened on the Way to the Broadcast Booth

The highlight of our schoolyard games was when the Good Humor ice cream truck would jingle its way to us. It was operated by a jolly gentleman named Sam, always dressed in his white Good Humor uniform, complete with a black-brimmed white cap. We would serenade him with "Sam, Sam the ice cream man" as we eagerly awaited our chocolate-coated ice cream bars and creamsicles. When he drove off, we would all yell "See you next time, Sam!" He would jingle his bells and disappear down the tree-lined street.

We always wondered what happened to Sam in the winter. Did he drive his Good Humor truck to Florida and sell his ice cream down there? It was one of the great mysteries of our youth.

Another haven was a wide, smoothly paved street called Ocean Avenue. From Friday after school until Sunday at sundown, that's where you would find my friends and me, playing our beloved roller hockey.

Ocean Avenue was right next to the Atlantic Ocean. We couldn't have asked for a more scenic backdrop. The best part about Ocean Avenue? It was a dead-end street, which meant there was very little traffic to interrupt our games. If a car ever did come through, we would all yell "Car, car!" and pull our homemade goals to the curb, then slide them back when the coast was clear.

Our own residence was like a mini sports complex. We lived in a comfortable two-story brick house with a backyard perfectly sized for playing catch. (In Brooklyn, we'd say "have a catch.") We also had a small area that could pass for a dugout, which was great when it rained. I would conduct rain delay interviews, just like the pros did on TV. During rain delays, the play-by-play announcer would toss it down to the dugout for interviews. In our backyard, I would be the announcer, chatting with my neighborhood pals who were posing as players. Even then, I was sharpening my interviewing skills.

The front of our house had steps leading up to the door, tailor made for stoopball. We used a Spaldeen, a pink rubber ball with a lively bounce. You would throw the ball toward the stoop, aiming for

My First Broadcast Booth

just the right point that would catapult it back over your head toward the street. We set rules for a single, double, and triple. If the ball reached the sidewalk on the other side of the street, it was a home run.

We also used a Spaldeen for stickball, which was similar to baseball, except we used a broomstick instead of a bat and played it on pavement, not grass. We used white chalk to lay out the baselines and bases.

I lived in a sports lover's paradise, a utopia for a sprouting sportscaster.

* * *

My fascination with sports and announcing was boundless.

On school nights, I would lie awake, listening to late games on my transistor radio under the covers and fantasizing about someday being in an arena or stadium, doing play-by-play.

Once when my earplug fell out of the jack and the radio suddenly blasted at full volume, both my parents came storming into my room. They just glared down at me with arms folded, then scolded me for staying up so late on a school night. The moment they left, I went right back to listening to the radio under the covers.

During more reasonable hours, I would tune in out-of-town broadcasts on my parents' radio set in the dining room. The signal was so clear, particularly at night. I felt like a safe cracker, delicately turning the dial in anxious anticipation of hearing the various announcers.

I was mesmerized by hockey. There was something special about the language and cadence of the play-by-play calls. Each broadcast was like a symphony.

I would hear the distinctive sound of Foster Hewitt calling a Toronto Maple Leaf's goal with his catchphrase, "He shoots, he scores!" I'd twist the knob slightly, and there was dulcet-toned Lloyd Pettit singing out, "Shot and a goal" in a Chicago Black Hawks game.

A Funny Thing Happened on the Way to the Broadcast Booth

Then, it was the velvet-throated Danny Gallivan calling the action for the Montreal Canadiens, shouting his trademark "A canonating drive!" I didn't recognize the players' names when I stumbled upon WOWO in Fort Wayne, Indiana. Had I discovered a parallel universe? No, it was minor league hockey, with the unique voice of Bob Chase announcing for the Fort Wayne Komets.

I would listen to these play-by-play masters almost every night, religiously.

* * *

When I wasn't listening to radio sports, I was watching television news. Weekday evenings, I was glued to Walter Cronkite or Huntley and Brinkley. I would closely study and analyze their styles and mannerisms.

I once had a substitute teacher in elementary school named Mrs. Blakeman. She assigned us to read an article in the newspaper and, the following day, we had to get up in front of the class to give a synopsis of the story. When it was my turn, I presented it as if I was anchoring a newscast. Normally shy in school, I was suddenly filled with confidence. Mrs. Blakeman and the class ate it up. I remember how gratifying that experience was. It made me want to do more of the same. I'll never forget Mrs. Blakeman for that assignment. She had a profound impact on my life.

While I was no different than any other kid in Brooklyn during those years, I was fortunate to know at a very young age exactly what I wanted to do when I grew up.

I knew, however, that despite my zeal, becoming a successful sports announcer was not guaranteed. It would entail hard work and sacrifice.

Growing up in Brooklyn and attending our homemade sportscasting "school" provided me with an extraordinary springboard for my career. I learned so much simply by being around my two older brothers. I couldn't have asked for better training in broadcasting. Everything, from turning down the sound on the TV and doing the play-by-play ourselves, to announcing ping-pong, to being immersed in a sports-crazy environment, paid dividends.

A Funny Thing Happened on the Way to the Broadcast Booth

What's in a Name?

My most traumatic childhood experience occurred in the fifth grade at P.S. 195. It was 1961 and I was ten.

My hand trembled as I reached out to give my teacher, Miss Shaughnessy, a note. Miss Shaughnessy was a tall, imposing woman. On occasion, she would show up in the classroom in full uniform, as she was not only a teacher, but also a member of the Women's Army Corps.

Miss Shaughnessy took my mother's hand-written note from me. I didn't know exactly what the note said, but I knew the subject matter. Sitting at her desk, Miss Shaughnessy took a few moments to read it to herself.

Then she stood up, dwarfing my pint-sized frame, and walked over to the front of the classroom, near the large black chalkboard. I was still standing by her desk, frozen with fear. She then motioned for me to come to her side. Head down, I shuffled my way to a spot alongside Miss Shaughnessy. I was terribly shy, and it was excruciating to be the center of attention. The entire class of about thirty pupils sat at their little desks, all eyes fixed on me. Each of my classmates seemed to have his or her head tilted at an angle, with looks of bewilderment. The room now fell deathly silent. I couldn't understand what Miss Shaughnessy was doing. Then she said, "Class, I have an announcement to make. Steve has a new name."

My classmates stared at me, motionless, jaws dropped. This was a first, not only for me but, I would wager, for every single kid in that classroom.

Who changes their name, and when someone does, who expects the teacher to announce it in front of the whole class? I thought when I went up to her desk to hand her the note that she would simply read it, and I'd go back and sit down at my desk and we would start our lessons for the day.

Then there's this question: Were my classmates wondering if I had changed my first name or my last name? Was I, from this day forward, to be addressed as George or Pete or Larry, rather than Steve?

I had no idea how to react. Should I do or say something, or do I continue to stand there, staring down at my feet?

Finally, Miss Shaughnessy ended the drama. She said, "Class, Steve's new last name is Albert."

As the seconds ticked by and beads of sweat formed on my forehead, I started to hear a faint sound. One of my classmates began to clap, a slow, rhythmic hand clap. Then another classmate started to clap. Before I knew it, the entire classroom, in what I can only guess was a spontaneous gesture of friendship and support, burst into wild applause. It broke the tension, and I was able to take a deep breath and walk back to my desk with a big smile and my head held high. Miss Shaughnessy smiled too and joined in the celebration.

As uncomfortably as it started, I look back on that day with warmth and fondness. In a way, Miss Shaughnessy brought me out of my shell and made me realize I didn't need to always be just

What's in a Name?

another face in the crowd. To this day, I haven't a clue as to who initiated the applause in my fifth-grade classroom, but let me just say to you now if you're out there . . . thank you from the bottom of my heart for transforming a very awkward moment into a cherished memory.

* * *

Why did I need to give that note to my teacher?

Well, one night, a couple of hours after dinner, my mother and father called my two brothers and me back to the dining room table and asked us to sit down.

My dad took the lead. He looked at us and said, "Fellas, I want to make life easier for you."

My brothers and I looked at each other with expressions that said, "What on earth is he talking about?"

He continued, "Fellas, our last name, Aufrichtig, isn't the easiest name to pronounce, right?" In unison, we exclaimed, "Right!"

Then he said, "I have a feeling about you three. Someday, you'll all need a last name that's easier for people to pronounce."

The three of us again looked at each other, only this time with a slight glint in our eyes.

"So, your mother and I," my dad continued, "went through the entire Brooklyn telephone book, and we came up with a new name, a name that will be simpler for you and everybody to say."

Now, the three of us were wide eyed and overflowing with curiosity. With all due respect to our original European surname, and with complete respect for our relatives who bear that name, we were pretty frustrated that people constantly mispronounced it and had no idea how to spell it.

"So, fellas," my father went on. "Our new last name is going to be Albert."

That's how it happened. Just like that. It was a pretty bold move. My parents had chutzpah.

I later found out that my father's number one choice was the name Rich, because it was the middle four letters of our original last name. However, my mother wanted a name that also started with the letter *A*, mainly because she was so accustomed to being first in line.

Guess who won that debate? My dad gave in to keep peace, and they came to the conclusion that Albert would be our new surname. My brothers and I didn't have much say in the matter, but we were all relieved that we wouldn't have to explain to people how to pronounce our last name anymore.

My father went through the legal process, and within a few days, we were the Albert family—Alida, Max, Marv, Al, and Steve Albert.

It felt strange at first, but we got used to it, and so did our friends and extended family. The name change seemed to mark a change in our lives, transforming our amateur announcing to something that we could do as professionals. We will always be Aufrichtigs, but from that moment on, we were the Albert sportscasting brothers.

Mom, Dad, and Brooklyn

My mother, Alida, was not a sports fan. She gave birth to three sportscasters.

My father, Max, enjoyed sports, but certainly not to the extent that his sons did while growing up and beyond.

One of the earliest memories I have of my mom is when she took me to school for the very first time. It was kindergarten at P.S. 195, just around the corner from where we lived. I was six years old, and I can remember how terrified I was. Today, we would call it separation anxiety. After she dropped me off and left, I couldn't stop crying. I mean loud, unabashed bawling.

Perhaps I knew what was coming. It was called sixteen more years of school—maybe that's the real reason I cried like a baby.

As I noted in an earlier chapter, when I was about seven, my mother took Al and me to the movies in downtown Brooklyn for my first moviegoing experience. The film was called *At War with the Army*, and it starred Dean Martin and Jerry Lewis. I remember sitting there with my buttered popcorn, roaring with laughter. It was the first time I had seen Jerry Lewis on screen, and I was hooked. It may have been the single greatest day of my life up to that point.

My mom was more into the arts. That's not to say that she didn't give sports the old college try. One of my fondest recollections is of the time when I was about fifteen years old and she took me to a Mets game at Shea Stadium in Flushing, Queens. She knew that the Dodgers, my favorite team, were in town. I didn't ask her to go, it was all her idea.

It was a beautiful, sunshiny day. I remember the pregame ceremony. The Dodgers' acclaimed relief pitcher Ron Perranoski was being honored by his hometown of Fairlawn, New Jersey. The Fairlawn High School Marching Band serenaded Ron on the field. My mother probably would have been a lot happier at a Carnegie Hall concert or the opera at Lincoln Center, but she made this special effort to share in something that I liked. It was a loving gesture and one of the few live sporting events my mom ever attended.

Perhaps what I remembered most about her at the game was that she brought her knitting with her. She was the only person in the stands who was knitting. She may not have remembered the specifics of that game, but I think she made a lot of progress on that sweater. Who knows? Extra innings might have produced a matching scarf.

Seriously, I appreciated what she did that day and it made a huge impression on me. Not only that, I think she actually enjoyed the experience, which made our outing even more meaningful to me.

My mother was a traditional post-World War II stay-at-home mom, but once in a while she would help out in my father's grocery store. She was a wonderful homemaker and an excellent cook. She stuck primarily to basic dishes, which was right up my father's alley. I never saw him vary his menu much, if at all. He was strictly a meat and potatoes guy. Forget sushi or Indian food.

My mom's go-to dinners were roast beef and meat loaf, but I always rushed home from playing outside when I knew she was making her famous baked chicken, seasoned with Kellogg's Corn Flakes. Her salmon croquettes were also delicious. The secret to her croquettes was yogurt. Sorry mom—I guess I let the cat out of the bag.

The only thing I refused to eat were cooked peas. She knew I hated them, yet for some mysterious reason, they frequently appeared as a side dish. Each time that happened, I would say to her, "Ma, you know I can't stand peas." She would always shoot back, "How do you know, if you don't taste them?" I'd reply, "I just know." Then she'd say, "All I am saying, is give peas a chance." Sorry, I made that last part up. I couldn't resist.

I appreciated my mother Alida Albert's (right) resolve and quirky sense of humor.

Occasionally, she took the night off. That meant Swanson's TV Dinners. The package was actually shaped like a TV set. The fried chicken and turkey were my top picks, and there was nothing better than the apple cobbler for dessert.

My mother was a strong-willed person. After Marv was born, her doctor told her not to have any more children. She was informed that health problems could arise if she went down that road again. Despite the sobering words of warning, she produced not one, but two more sportscasters—I mean children. Thankfully, there were no repercussions. Had my mother followed doctor's orders, Marv would have been a solo act in the Little Room.

I believe I inherited that determination from my mother, not to mention a quirky sense of humor with a hint of sarcasm. Okay, more than a hint.

My maternal grandparents, Morris and Aranka Kahn, emigrated from Hungary to the United States. My grandfather had been a jeweler. I never knew my grandmother, as she passed away when I was an infant. My grandfather was a dashing silver-haired gentleman who sported a mustache. Tragically, my mother lost her younger brother, Alfred, during World War II. Alfie, as my mom called him, was an army pilot whose plane was shot down in the South Pacific. I don't think my mother ever recovered from that heartbreak. She seldom talked about it, and I never pressed her on it. He was a handsome lad, judging from photos. I also recall some thoughtful letters he wrote to a very young Marv that our mom would read to him. I wish I had gotten to meet my Uncle Alfie.

Despite the fact we were not always on the same wavelength, my mother never tried to stop my brothers and me from pursuing our dreams. She didn't understand sports or how sports affected the lives of so many people, but she saw how invested we were, even at early ages, in the idea of becoming sportscasters. Eventually, she realized it wasn't a passing fancy. My mom would joke about it from time to time, saying things like "Couldn't we throw in just one doctor or lawyer?" Nope. She was stuck with three future sportscasters.

As Marv began to gain prominence and Al and I were coming into our own, my mom would sometimes be asked how it felt to be the mother of three sportscasters. Her stock answer was "The best part of being the mother of the Albert brothers is always knowing where my sons are. I just turn on the TV."

When my brothers and I became more established and recognized, doing play-by-play and appearing on the six and eleven o'clock news in New York, we noticed that our mother's disposition began to change. She became more accepting of our career choices. We found out that she was suddenly the envy of all her friends and had become somewhat of a celebrity in the neighborhood. People would come up and congratulate her at social functions, some even asked for her autograph.

I guess it finally hit her: Her sons might actually be making their marks in the world.

* * *

My father, Max, was a man of humility who had a strong work ethic, attributes I always admired in him. As I got older, although I knew he wasn't an expert in broadcasting, he was the one I called after most broadcasts. I valued his judgment and plain old common sense.

Mathematics came easily to my dad, but not to me. I was more like my mom in that regard. My mother and I were more into history and English. Algebra and trigonometry were like foreign languages to me, which irked my dad. He couldn't comprehend my struggles through high school, and his attempts at tutoring me only led to frustration for both of us. My father's explanations went in one ear and out the other. Nothing registered. My dad was beside himself, and I was on the threshold of an emotional breakdown. Then, one day, out of nowhere, the oddest thing happened. It all snapped into place. Incredibly, in a crucial end-of-the-term math exam, I scored a high grade, an 89.

I admired my father Max Albert's (right) humility, wisdom, and work ethic.

I couldn't wait for my father to come home from work so I could show him the test result. He was thrilled beyond belief—I hadn't seen him that happy in a long time. I think he felt bad later in life that he was so stern with me. At the time, it was agonizing, but I understood as I matured. He was old school. These days, they'd call it tough love.

That's not to say my dad didn't have a soft side. My father was born in 1916, the same year John F. Kennedy was born. I thought that was cool since JFK was one of my idols while I was growing up.

When I was about eight years old, I stayed home from school one morning with a bad cold. I was watching *The Today Show*. The guest was Senator John Kennedy from Massachusetts. It was the first time I had ever seen him interviewed. He came off as smart and funny, with a sort of self-deprecating sense of humor. I could tell immediately he had the "It" factor. I even did a book report on him, sketching his likeness on the cover.

Then I watched his debate with Richard Nixon. That sealed it for me. Kennedy was tanned and relaxed. Nixon was sweaty and tense. If that debate had only been heard on the radio, there might have been a different outcome in the 1960 election. Even as a kid, I recognized the power of television.

On the night of the election, it was getting late, and my father said I had to go to sleep. After all, it was a school night. I asked my dad, "Please leave a note on my bedroom door, telling me who won."

When I woke up the next morning, there it was, an 8½" x 11" piece of paper taped to my door with two very memorable words: "Kennedy won." I jumped for joy.

To this day, I associate John F. Kennedy with that note my father posted on my bedroom door.

My dad was a child of the Great Depression, circumstances that would make anyone judicious in spending their hard-earned money. However, he was anything but cheap. In fact, he was very generous. My father never hesitated to take the family out for special meals. He would tip not only the waiters, but the busboys as well. He never turned down a panhandler on the street, and he was always there for me if I ever needed a few bucks, as long as it was for a nonfrivolous reason. He was a practical person, another characteristic I admired. My dad also put three boys through college, never once asking for a dime back.

My father and his brother Ted owned and operated a family-style grocery store on Brighton 3rd Street, under the train tracks. It was called Aufrichtig's.

My dad's parents, Nathan and Fanny, came over from Poland. They settled in Brighton Beach, where my grandfather started the store. My father said that when he was a child, Grandpa Nathan was strict. He must have mellowed with age. My grandfather was wonderful to my brothers and me. He had an easy smile and a gleeful laugh.

My grandmother passed away when I was very young, but I have fond memories of her as being kind and sweet.

A Funny Thing Happened on the Way to the Broadcast Booth

I'll never forget the endless stairway to the door of my grandparents' modest one-bedroom apartment, which was located above the store. I was always out of breath when I finally reached the top. I felt like I had scaled the Matterhorn and wanted to plant a flag.

When Grandpa Nathan retired, the store was turned over to my father and uncle. My dad had his heart set on a career in finance or economics, but the family business took precedence. He never brought it up, but there were times when I could tell he had some regrets. That was a different generation, and many people kept things to themselves. They didn't discuss personal feelings as freely as they do today.

My father and Uncle Ted worked their tails off in that store for years, putting in long hours, six days a week, Monday through Saturday.

The best part of being a grocer's son was closing time. Occasionally, I would accompany my mother when she drove into Brighton Beach to pick up my dad at around 7:00 p.m. As he was turning out the lights, my father would tell me to take what I would like off the shelves before we left for home. I went straight for my favorites, like Wise potato chips, Goldenberg's Peanut Chews, and Mallomars. As a kid, there was nothing better than a glass of cold milk and Mallomars, a graham cracker topped with marshmallow and coated in chocolate.

My dad would freeze boxes of Mallomars over the winter so he could sell them during the summer. Aufrichtig's was the only store in Brighton Beach, maybe in Brooklyn, that had Mallomars all year round.

One summer, my father persuaded me to work in the store part time. I think he purposely did that to dissuade me from ever working there full time in the future. My dad was a man of wisdom, and if that experience didn't solidify my sportscasting aspirations, nothing would have.

One morning when I was working in the store, an elderly woman shuffled in. She said to my Uncle Ted and me, "I'm very tired. Do you mind if I rest here for a moment?" My uncle said, "Of course, lady" and immediately placed a wooden crate upright on the floor so she could sit down.

At 7:00 p.m., my father and uncle turned out the lights to leave. They noticed that still sitting there on the crate, in the dark, was the lady who had come into the store in the morning. It must have been so busy all day that nobody had noticed she was still there. My father and uncle gently helped her up and then out to the sidewalk, where she smiled, said "Thank you," and went on her merry way. If they hadn't taken one last look around, she might have sat in the store all night. At least she wouldn't have gone hungry.

When my father came home from work, he would sit at the head of the dinner table with an ice-cold Schaeffer Beer, "the one beer to have when you're having more than one." After dinner, we would turn on the TV and watch our favorite shows. Back then, there were only seven channels, and you actually had to get up to change the channel.

My earliest recollection of watching TV was a CBS children's show on Saturday morning called *Winky Dink and You*, which featured a magic drawing screen. In fact, it was a piece of vinyl plastic stuck to the TV screen on which you could draw with crayons. Occasionally I would forget to apply the vinyl plastic and just drew on the screen. My parents were not amused.

My father and I loved *The Honeymooners* and *The Phil Silvers Show*. My dad had a high, cackling laugh, and his howling could be heard in Bensonhurst. On Sunday nights, my folks and I religiously tuned in to *The Ed Sullivan Show*. I was mesmerized by Topo Gigio, Johnny Puleo and the Harmonica Gang, and the comedians, like Nichols and May, Stiller and Meara, and Moms Mabley. On certain nights, my parents would let me stay up late to watch Steve Allen and Jack Paar in the early days of late-night television. I was hooked on the game shows, like *I've Got a Secret*, *What's My Line*, and *To Tell the Truth*. Among Westerns, *The Lone Ranger* and *The Rifleman* were my personal favorites. Then there was this: "Faster than a speeding bullet! More powerful than a locomotive! Able to leap tall buildings in a single bound! Look! Up in the sky! It's a bird! It's a plane! It's Superman!" I remember how excited I was when my father bought a color TV. Finally, *Bonanza*'s Ponderosa in living color!

All of these shows affected me greatly, but before the term "Must See TV" even existed, I never missed an episode of *Abbott and Costello* or *The Soupy Sales Show*.

That said, there was one other program that really stood out. When I was about eight or nine, my dad and I would watch the Friday night fights together on our black and white TV. It was the golden age of boxing, and the broadcast was called *The Gillette Cavalcade of Sports Friday Night Fights*.

This was my introduction to boxing. Every telecast featured storied fighters like Carmen Basilio, Gene Fullmer, Sugar Ray Robinson, Emile Griffith, Floyd Patterson, and more. I was fascinated by the unmistakable voices of ring announcer Johnny Addie and blow-by-blow man Don Dunphy. Little did my father know that the little squirt sitting next to him back then would someday join those two legends in the Boxing Hall of Fame.

* * *

I have vivid memories of my father taking the whole family to our favorite restaurant, Lundy's, in Sheepshead Bay. It was a Brooklyn landmark that specialized in seafood and chops, and it was extraordinarily large.

Lundy's had several incarnations and, unfortunately, closed its doors for the last time in 2007. They did not take reservations, and it was always so crowded that patrons would stand and wait behind the chairs of people who were still eating. Arguments and fights would sporadically break out as people hovered over those trying to finish their meals. Lundy's food was to die for, but it wasn't worth losing your life over it. Then again, their mouthwatering hot biscuits were almost worth going to war over.

On Sundays, we would pile into my dad's maroon DeSoto and make the short pilgrimage to Nathan's in Coney Island. Nathan's hot dogs and french fries—need I say more?

Another favorite was Kwai Fong in Brighton Beach, for the best Chinese food in Brooklyn. I always ordered the number one combination platter of chicken chow mein, fried rice, and an egg roll. One time, my brother Al loaded my egg roll with Kwai Fong's choice sauce and said to me, "Try this. You'll love it." Like a good kid brother, I took a big bite. It turns out the choice sauce was a fiery hot chili sauce that nearly sent me through the roof. My mouth was on fire, and everyone at the table was crying with laughter. I was just crying.

There was a little hole-in-the-wall shop across the street from the El in Brighton Beach called Mrs. Stahl's Knishes. For the uninitiated, a knish is a traditional Jewish delicacy that consists of various fillings, such as mashed potatoes, kasha, onion, ground meat, sweet potatoes, spinach, cheese, or cherry cheese, covered with dough. I was a potato knish guy. They were heavenly. Piping hot Mrs, Stahl's knishes were great all year round but particularly sublime on cold winter days.

Whenever we returned home from a trip to Manhattan (which we always called the "City"), we would decide which subway station to get off at based on what kind of food we wanted. Delmar Pizzeria was right next to the train station in Sheepshead Bay, so if we had a yen for a slice of incredibly good cheesy pizza, we would get off at Sheepshead Bay, then hop on the B1 bus into Manhattan Beach. If we craved a knish, we'd jump out at the Brighton Beach station, then get on the B21 bus to Manhattan Beach.

Food, glorious food! It was such an integral part of my childhood.

You would think that my childhood obsession with food would have turned me into a "foodie" as an adult. To the contrary, I'm now happiest with a good straight-up turkey sandwich. I have sportscaster Rich Ackerman to thank for this. Rich (who was a summer camp bunkmate of my nephew, Kenny Albert, and became a family friend) was always ordering a turkey sandwich whenever we ate together. Now it's become my go-to sandwich.

* * *

Every so often, my father would drive us up to the Catskills for a long weekend. The rides themselves were memorable, not necessarily for good reasons.

My father was an overly cautious driver, so every trip seemed endless. What should have been a two-and-a-half-hour drive could take double that. My brother Al and I would invariably get into a fight in the back seat. My mother would lose it, then my father would yell, "Okay, I'm going to turn this car around if you boys don't stop!" Al and I would look at each other, as if to say, "We can't take being in this car for much longer," and the two of us would zip our lips the rest of the way.

Our customary destination was Grossinger's Catskill Resort Hotel. We loved to ice-skate and go tobogganing. On some weekends, the hotel would stage barrel jumping competitions on their gigantic skating rink that were sometimes televised on ABC's *Wide World of Sports*.

I also got to see some legendary comedians performing their routines in the Borscht Belt, like Totie Fields and Henny Youngman. They were insanely funny, and it was great to sit next to my father, who, as I mentioned earlier, had this infectious high-pitched laugh. The comedians loved my dad because his chortling would cause a ripple of others' laughter to spread like wildfire throughout the massive Grossinger's nightclub.

For me, the best part of Grossinger's was the television set that sat at the front of a giant ballroom facing row after row of chairs. It was a color TV.

Mom, Dad, and Brooklyn

My parents (back row left) and I (front row left) on the ice with neighborhood friends at Grossinger's Catskill Resort Hotel.

I couldn't wait until Saturday night, because that's when the Rangers played road games. They wore their traveling blue shirts with red hockey pants. Color TV had not yet been perfected, so the colors would bleed over onto the ice, which didn't bother me one bit.

While my parents and all the other guests were dining or dancing at the nightclub, I would sit in a chair in the front row of the ginormous room all by myself, glued to the Rangers game, with Win Elliott behind the mic.

On occasion, Al would join me, and after the game we would go to Grossinger's malt shop to get egg creams, one of the greatest beverages ever created. It consists of milk, seltzer, and the all-important Fox's U-Bet chocolate syrup. Good times.

A Funny Thing Happened on the Way to the Broadcast Booth

All dressed up for dinner in Grossinger's dining room with family and friends (from top left, Al, mom, dad, and me).

* * *

I was fortunate to have parents who, despite not always understanding what their three sons were planning to do when they grew up, gave us the freedom to pursue our goals. At times, it could not have been easy for them. I can only imagine the conversations they may have had about my brothers and me, but they never put pressure on us to do something else. I may not have fully appreciated that when I was a little boy, but I sure did later in life.

I lost my mom in 1990, during my first year announcing for the Golden State Warriors. Too young. She was only seventy-one. I hope she was proud of what we had accomplished. Had she lived longer, who knows, maybe she would even have become a sports fan. I can dream, can't I?

Mom, Dad, and Brooklyn

I got closer to my dad as he got on in years. There's something about the bond between a son and his father.

My dad treated me to my first live fight card when I was seventeen. It was March 4, 1968, at Madison Square Garden. Heavyweights Joe Frazier and Buster Mathis were the headliners. Our seats were way up in the last row. I was in heaven, literally and figuratively.

At the time, Grandpa Nathan, my father's dad, was in failing health and staying with us. Before the main event, my father said he wanted to call my mother to see how my grandfather was doing.

About ten minutes later, my father returned to his seat and stared straight ahead. I asked, "How is grandpa?"

My dad said, "He passed away."

I said, "What? He died? Let's go home!"

My father said, "No, not yet. I want to see the fight. We'll go home right after Frazier-Mathis." That's just the way my father was. He took care of everything and made all the arrangements as soon as we got home.

Thirty-two years later, in April 2000, I had a Showtime boxing telecast in China. The main event was a heavyweight bout between Andrew Golota and Marcus Rhode. I flew twenty-plus hours to Guangzhou, arriving bleary eyed at about six o'clock in the morning.

The first person to greet me in the hotel lobby was the local boxing promoter, a young Chinese man. He introduced himself and said, "Please sit down. I've got to tell you something."

I said, "Yes?"

He said, "Your father passed away."

I had a sinking feeling in my gut when he told me to sit down, and when he uttered those words, they seemed to come at me in slow motion. At this point, I thought I was having a bad dream and wanted to wake up.

He asked me if I was all right. I said, "Yes, I'm okay." I wasn't really. The combination of the news and the jet lag made me queasy.

A Funny Thing Happened on the Way to the Broadcast Booth

My mind started to race. Then, I flashed back to the night my father took me to my first fight show, the night my father's father had passed away.

I had a few minutes before I had to return to the airport and went up to my room to freshen up. When I got there, everything just hit me. I suddenly realized that for the first time in my life, I had no parents. I felt like the aging comic Buddy Young Jr., played by Billy Crystal in the movie *Mr. Saturday Night*. After his mother died, he said to his brother, "We're orphans."

I flew another twenty-plus hours, from China back to New York, which gave me lots of time to ponder the parallels between my father's and grandfather's passings. My father was at a boxing match when his father died. I was in China to announce a boxing match when my father died. My grandfather lived to see his sons succeed in the family business. My father, who was eighty-four when he passed, lived to see his sons succeed in the family business.

Max Albert and sons (from left, Max, me, Marv and Al Albert)

Marv, Al, and Me

When not occupied with becoming a sportscaster, I was often in my room developing cartoon characters. I drew all the time, even creating my own comic books. My two older brothers were convinced I was going to be a professional cartoonist when I grew up. I guess I should take that as a compliment. They were tough critics.

As I got older, my mother thought I was going to be an architect. She was so excited because I started to construct model ballparks of Yankee Stadium and Fenway Park out of cardboard. I was fascinated with those structures, often studying pictures of them in books and magazines. When my mock stadiums were completed, I would store them under my bed. Most old stadiums become parking lots. Mine gathered dust. It turned out to be nothing more than an adolescent phase, and never went beyond that, much to my mom's dismay.

While I did enjoy those other creative endeavors, my heart was always in broadcasting. For me, there was no plan B.

Al, the middle brother, however, did flirt with another career. Aside from announcing sports, Al had set his sights on playing professional hockey.

Marv? When he was born and the doctor slapped his bottom, instead of crying, he yelled, "Yesss! And it counts!" There was no question about the path he would take. As a youngster, he started his own radio station in the house, with the call letters WMPA, which stood for Marvin Philip Aufrichtig. He would do imaginary broadcasts from his room. We finally got him to stop about five years ago.

Marv's only diversion was when he took piano lessons. In seven years of lessons, Marv learned to play two songs: "Malaguena" and "Autumn Leaves." His teacher was a gentleman named Mr. Carlin. Marv told me that the best thing about piano lessons was Mr. Carlin's mimeograph machine, which he would use to print out sports reports for Lincoln High School. My mother always wondered why Marv came home from his piano lessons with blue ink all over his fingers. Marv would tell her that Mr. Carlin had blue piano keys.

Al also played a musical instrument, the accordion. We couldn't get enough of his rendition of "Lady of Spain."

Me, I played the saxophone and the clarinet. I was so bad that my music teacher once fell asleep in the middle of my lesson. I left him his money and tiptoed out of his house.

I played in the Lincoln High School Marching Band. We looked like the band in *Animal House* that marches into the alley and straight into a wall. The silver lining was that it morphed into a job as the public address announcer for football games.

When Marv was at Syracuse University, he would bring home tape reels of his work on the air. When I listened to them, he sounded so advanced for his age. Marv called the basketball games for the Syracuse Orangemen on the campus radio station, WAER, cutting his teeth on the sport that brought him the most acclaim. In addition, while in college Marv turned pro by announcing baseball games for the Triple-A Syracuse Chiefs and by spinning records as a fast-talking rock and roll disc jockey, broadcasting under the name of Lance Scott on WOLF radio.

My folks and I took a trip to Syracuse one weekend to visit Marv. We got tickets to a Syracuse-St. John's basketball game that Marv was announcing. I was not an autograph seeker, mainly out of shyness, but I worked up the courage to approach legendary St. John's coach Joe Lapchick before the game. He graciously obliged. The Johnnies coach was a tall man, and he towered over a little runt like me. I held onto that autograph for years.

After scoring what was my first-ever autograph, I was brimming with confidence and decided to go for another. During the game, I walked behind the Syracuse bench, tapped Ernie Davis on the shoulder, and said, "Excuse me, Mr. Davis, may I please have your autograph?" The football star, who also suited up for basketball, turned around, looked at me, and said politely, "Sorry son, we're not allowed to sign autographs during the game." I was crestfallen, but I understood, and I got to tell all my friends that I actually spoke to Ernie Davis. That was just as good as, if not better than, an autograph.

Syracuse had a winning football team when Marv attended the school, and Ernie Davis was the team's big star. In fact, Marv and Ernie were fraternity brothers, members of Sigma Alpha Mu. Ernie was the first African American to win the Heisman Trophy and went on to become the number one overall pick in the 1962 NFL draft by the then-Washington Redskins, who immediately traded him to the Cleveland Browns. That same year, before ever playing in his first pro game, Ernie Davis died of leukemia at the age of twenty-three. I was crushed.

* * *

A Funny Thing Happened on the Way to the Broadcast Booth

I was twelve when Marv had an opportunity to call his first Knicks game on the radio. He was twenty-one. He had transferred from Syracuse to New York University as a senior to work at WCBS radio as a writer and fill-in announcer for Marty Glickman, the renowned voice of the New York Knicks. Marty was a god in New York. His distinctive sound and his crisp, clean descriptions of Giants football and Knicks basketball on the radio were unparalleled. On top of that, he was credited with devising the court geography that all basketball play-by-play announcers use to this day to describe the action. Marty would insert the location of shots in his description of the action with vivid phrases such as "he shoots from the top of the key," "he dribbles across the midcourt line," and "he drives down the lane." Marty was a broadcasting icon, and all three of us looked up to him with reverence.

As if Marty's impressive broadcasting credentials weren't enough, he also had been a football and track star at James Madison High School in Brooklyn. Later, he was a collegiate standout at Syracuse. He also made the U.S. Olympic track team and would have participated in the 1936 Berlin Summer Olympics if not for Adolph Hitler's anti-Jewish policies. In what is now Olympic folklore, Marty and his Jewish American teammate, Sam Stoller, were removed at the last minute from the four-hundred-meter relay and replaced by Jesse Owens and Ralph Metcalfe, who easily captured the gold medal.

While Marty profoundly influenced us all, his biggest impact was on Marv, who soon became his understudy. One Saturday night in January of 1963, Marv received a phone call at our home in Manhattan Beach from Marty. He was in Paris, France, on business, and told Marv that he couldn't make it back in time for the next Knicks broadcast because he was stuck in a severe snowstorm. He asked Marv if he would announce the game, to be played the next afternoon in Boston. Marty was obviously confident that Marv could do the job.

My brother Marv (right) with his mentor Marty Glickman (left). Marv's first full-time sportscasting job was at WHN Radio in New York.

When Marv told us the news, we were stunned. After a few minutes, shock turned to glee. Marv, meanwhile, seemed quite composed. His demeanor was always reserved and low key, but let's try to put this in perspective. Marv was still in college, but he had been asked by the incomparable Marty Glickman to take his place and announce a game between the Knicks and the Celtics on the fabled parquet floor of the Boston Garden in a matter of hours.

My parents were in disbelief. They were unassuming, unpretentious people, and this sudden development was overwhelming.

Marv asked my parents if he could take Al, then sixteen, to assist him and serve as his statistician. My parents said Al could go, and I too wanted to take part in this once-in-a-lifetime adventure. I had a gut feeling that this was going to be the start of something big, and I fiercely wanted to be there with my brothers. My parents said I was too young to make the trip. They were adamant and wouldn't allow me to go. I begged them. I promised I wouldn't leave Marv's and Al's sides for a second.

"Please let me go with them," I pleaded, but to no avail. It broke my heart. For years, I couldn't let go of my disappointment. Occasionally, I reminded my parents about it, much to their chagrin.

That night, my brothers departed on an eleven o'clock train, which arrived in Boston at 3:00 a.m. for Sunday afternoon's tip-off.

As if this trip wasn't stressful enough, when Marv and Al got to the Boston Garden, the security guards wouldn't let them in. They didn't believe Marv when he said he was there to broadcast the game for the Knicks. He looked too young. His stat man, Al, looked even younger. Following an angst-filled conversation, Marv convinced the crusty Boston Garden security people to contact a Knicks official, who verified that Marv was there to call the game.

Meanwhile, back home in Brooklyn, I needed to feel involved, so I called all my friends and told them to listen to the game. My brother was going to announce for the Knicks! He was sitting in for Marty Glickman!

Leading up to the game, I just tried to stay out of my parents' way. I was still brooding because they wouldn't let me tag along with my brothers, but I knew how edgy they were.

As the broadcast time drew closer, my parents and I huddled around the large radio in the living room. We turned it on and tuned in to WCBS, 880 on the dial. We were a bundle of nerves. My heart pounded as the minutes ticked toward game time.

Finally, the theme music came on, and we heard the crowd in the background. Then, for the first time on a Knicks radio broadcast, we heard "Hi everybody, this is Marv Albert filling in for Marty Glickman, and welcome to New York Knicks basketball." I saw the looks on my parents' faces. I think that first of all, they were relieved their boys had made it safely to Boston. Then there was the thrill of hearing their son on the air, and on such a high-profile platform! For me, hearing my brother's voice live on the radio for the first time was mind-blowing. I had heard tapes of him, but this was different. I knew how hard he had worked to reach this point.

As the Knicks-Celtics game got underway and Marv settled into his familiar staccato, rapid-fire play-by-play style, my parents beamed. My own smile stretched to Sheepshead Bay. I couldn't wait to go to school the next day to talk with my pals about my brother's first Knicks broadcast.

Legendary Brooklyn Dodgers executive Branch Rickey famously said, "Luck is the residue of design." Well, Marv's first Knicks broadcast was the product of hard work and an insatiable drive. That was the design part. The luck part was Marty Glickman's phone call from Paris.

I knew when I listened to Marv's first Knicks broadcast that it surely wasn't going to be his last. While his debut was memorable for all of us on Kensington Street, fans throughout New York truly came to appreciate his radio play-by-play during the Knicks' glorious championship run in 1969-70, as many of those games were either tape delayed or blacked out on television. That was when his career really took off. With his skills, national prominence was only a matter of time.

He would become one of the most popular and versatile announcers ever, calling hockey, football, and boxing from coast to coast.

But there is no denying that basketball play-by-play was his true calling. His legacy of thirty-seven years behind the mic for the Knicks on radio and television and as the voice of the NBA on NBC and TNT earned him a place among the immortals in the Basketball Hall of Fame. And it all began on that fateful January day in Boston.

As I noted earlier, I knew it was going to be the start of something big. I'm still miffed that I didn't get to go.

A Funny Thing Happened on the Way to the Broadcast Booth

* * *

When I was growing up in Brooklyn, the only NHL team in New York was the Rangers. Almost every kid in the neighborhood was a Rangers fan, as were my brothers and I. We played all the Brooklyn street games, but it was roller hockey that ruled. For Al and me, it was a religion.

Ice was not plentiful where we grew up. The only ice we could find was in a glass of Coca-Cola. We weren't in Canada, and we weren't blessed with ice rinks like some U.S. communities, so we did the next best thing. We played on asphalt.

Ocean Avenue was perfect because it was a wide, evenly paved street that offered a smooth skating surface. Al was an exceptional skater and goal scorer. He got so good that he moved up to an organized league in a nearby neighborhood called Kings Highway, where he played with the best players in Brooklyn. It seemed like my brother was always their leading scorer.

Al used to take me to the old Garden to see the Rangers. My favorite player was Gump Worsley, the Rangers' goaltender. I spent more time in the men's room than usual because they piped in the radio call and I could listen to Rangers announcer Jim Gordon.

Al especially liked going to see the Rangers play the Black Hawks. We would get there early for warmups, sneak downstairs from the cheap seats, and sit behind the Chicago goal, where my brother would study the silky-smooth moves of goaltender Glenn Hall. Watching the future hall of famer known as "Mr. Goalie" from that proximity was an education. Al analyzed him closely, like an aspiring young violinist picking up pointers from Jascha Heifetz.

Another time, before a game at the new Garden, we walked over to the hotel across the street where most of the visiting teams stayed while in New York. The Rangers were hosting the Montreal Canadiens that night, and we rode the elevator, hoping to catch a glimpse of one of our heroes.

We went up and down so many times, I got dizzy. When we had just about given up hope, the door slid open, and there he was, the man we worshipped, in our opinion the greatest goaltender who ever lived, his eminence, Jacques Plante.

In person, he was bigger than life. He looked like a movie star, impeccably dressed in a stylish suit, his dark hair carefully coiffed, his face deeply tanned. (I wondered, "How does someone living in Montreal in the winter have a tan?")

We couldn't believe it was him and couldn't wait to tell everyone at our next roller hockey game that we saw Jacques Plante, in the flesh.

* * *

As chronicled, Al had been a standout roller hockey player. He was determined to play ice hockey for Ohio University. The amazing thing is that while he was a high-flying scoring forward on the streets of Brooklyn, he had never played ice hockey competitively until college.

Because of his late start on the ice, his skating skills as a forward were not up to collegiate standards. But his quick reflexes would keep him on the ice as a goaltender. Over the next two years on the JV team, Al would hone his goalie skating and fundamental skills. He was a natural, and by his junior year found himself as the backup goalie on the varsity team.

Al, a radio and TV major, was already doing the Ohio basketball play-by-play on the college radio station. And so, with a little prodding, his understanding hockey coach, John McComb, allowed him to go up to the broadcast booth to announce the home hockey games on the school station. Al did his play-by-play fully uniformed in his complete hockey gear, including his bulky goalie pads and skates, should he ever be needed on the ice. I suspect the wise coach also found that this was a way to make more room on an overcrowded bench.

A Funny Thing Happened on the Way to the Broadcast Booth

It worked out well. That year, instead of being the seldom used backup languishing at the end of the bench, Al gained valuable hockey announcing experience, along with a great workout clomping up and down the two flights of stairs to the broadcast booth in his cumbersome goalie paraphernalia.

As a senior, Al would make no more trips to the broadcast booth, as he became the full-time starting goalie and went on to establish team records for wins, shutouts, and saves in a season. That was impressive enough for Al to be invited by New York Rangers general manager Emile Francis to the Rangers training camp.

I was home in Brooklyn, gearing up for my freshman year in college, when Al, who was also living at home, was notified of this incredible opportunity. A Rangers fan from Brooklyn getting a tryout with his hometown team? It sounded like something only a Hollywood screenwriter could dream up.

Al was all set to travel north to the Rangers training camp in Kitchener, Ontario. Marv, then the Rangers radio play-by-play announcer, wanted to go along to lend support, and he asked me if I would like to join them.

I said I wouldn't miss it for the world. (Perhaps he asked me to make up for the time I wasn't permitted to go with my brothers to Boston for Marv's first Knicks broadcast.) My parents, of course, were excited too, but somebody had to mind the store. What an adventure for me as I was about to enter college, what a treat for Marv as the team's radio voice, and what an experience for Al, who would be on the ice with players he idolized.

Marv and I got to Kitchener and walked into the arena on the opening day of training camp. The first thing I noticed was a giant portrait of Queen Elizabeth on one of the end zone walls. I didn't know she was a hockey fan.

As I looked down on the ice, there they were. All my favorite New York Rangers were skating around—Eddie Giacomin, Rod Gilbert, Jean Ratelle, Vic Hadfield, and Jim Neilson. And wait. What? Al?

My brother, on the ice trying out for our hometown New York Rangers?!?! As talented as he was, it seemed incomprehensible.

The ice was packed with players. Not only were the Rangers skating around, so were the Buffalo Bisons, the Rangers' top farm team from the American Hockey League, and other invitees like Al. Marv and I leaned forward and focused on the ice, looking for our brother. Simultaneously, we blurted out, "There's Al!"

My brother Al's official player photo at the New York Rangers training camp in 1968.

It was quite a rush to see him wearing a Rangers uniform, skating around with all those Rangers players, many of whom we grew up watching on TV. Years later, when I watched the movie *Rudy*, I had flashbacks of Al on the ice with the Rangers.

The NHL was predominantly Canadian back then. My brother was a local kid from Brooklyn, which was unheard of.

How was Al doing? After a session, he ran into the Rangers' coach, the legendary "Boom Boom" Geoffrion, who vigorously shook

A Funny Thing Happened on the Way to the Broadcast Booth

Al's hand and exclaimed in his heavy French-Canadian accent, "You, you, you, you, you, good!" To this day, Al has never washed that hand.

Our excitement came to an abrupt halt when, in one of the morning sessions, a Bison farmhand named Wayne Larkin collapsed on the ice in front of Al, who was in goal. Marv and I were sitting about halfway up the stands with Geoffrion when it happened. Boom Boom, as if shot from a cannon, hurdled over the seats down to the ice. They were unable to revive the player, and he died of a heart attack in the ambulance en route to the hospital. It left a pall over the camp, which was canceled for the rest of the day.

* * *

Oh, one other thing. Prior to reporting to the Rangers' camp, Al had received his draft notice to report to army basic training the following week. It was the height of the Vietnam War, but he couldn't pass up this once-in-a-lifetime opportunity with the Rangers. He stayed at the camp as long as he could before he had to report to Fort Leonard Wood in Missouri. He got to wear that Rangers uniform for only a few days.

Emile Francis, who was aware of the circumstances, was impressed with Al and was hoping to keep my brother in Kitchener, but Uncle Sam had first dibs. The dream was over and Al reported for duty as required, swapping his New York Rangers uniform for U.S. Army gear.

Following Al's army service, Emile Francis oversaw my brother's assignment to a minor league team, and his dream of an NHL career was fast-tracked. But, not as a goalie.

An inauspicious start on the ice in Toledo made Al realize that an NHL career would be more likely in the broadcast booth. And, as fate would have it, the team was serendipitously just finalizing a radio deal, and Al seamlessly moved behind the microphone as Toledo's play-by-play announcer. That went so well that two years later, Al did make it to the NHL as the voice of the expansion New York Islanders as well as with the ABA, doing play-by-play for the Nets, whose games were broadcast on the same station. That would ultimately lead Al to the national stage as the prime announcer for the USA Network's coverage of the NHL, the NBA, and the popular long-running *Tuesday Night Fights*.

So, an abbreviated professional hockey career turned into Al's long-term professional sportscasting career.

For me, while Al's Rangers "career" was short-lived, I'll always have that unforgettable image of my brother on the ice in a Rangers uniform.

A Funny Thing Happened on the Way to the Broadcast Booth

It's All Relative

Leon Wood was a first-round pick in 1984 who played six NBA seasons for six different teams. He was a member of the 1984 gold medal U.S. Olympic team coached by Bob Knight. He later became an NBA referee.

Leon was known as a tough competitor who loved to shoot from long range. In the 1986-87 season, Leon was traded to the Nets from the then-Washington Bullets.

When he came out to the floor at the Meadowlands Arena to warm up before his first game in a Nets uniform, I went over to introduce myself.

I shook his hand and said, "Hi Leon, I'm Steve Albert, the Nets TV play-by-play announcer."

He looked at me and said in a serious tone, "Are you any relation to your brother Marv?"

I had to think to myself for a second. Did he just say what I think he said? "Are you any *relation* to your *brother* Marv?"

I chuckled and said, "Yes, I guess I am."

I couldn't resist, so I went back to the pressroom and mentioned it to one of the writers. Wouldn't you know it? That made it into *Sports Illustrated*'s top quotes of the year.

From that moment on, every time I saw Leon, as a player and subsequently as a ref, we would look at each other and burst out laughing. We both knew exactly why.

Anyone who has ever grown up with older siblings knows that you will invariably be compared to each other. It comes with the territory. As three brothers, all passionately pursuing careers in the same profession, especially one as competitive as sportscasting, the comparisons were a regular occurrence.

You might think that this would cause sibling rivalry. The only place, however, where we showed any sign of a rivalry was when we played ping-pong, which became a mainstay in our lives. Even today, my brothers and I occasionally meet to play at an establishment called Spin in the Flatiron District of Manhattan. We still engage in mortal combat as we did as kids, but without the play-by-play accompaniment. We don't want to be spun out of Spin by the authorities.

During our careers, the three of us could not have been more supportive of one another. We felt that there were plenty of jobs to go around, although at times it seemed like Marv had most of them. Seriously, I can't remember one instance when my brothers and I even competed for the same position. If anything, we were always rooting for each other to succeed.

When we were kids? That was another story. Sometimes, Al would walk by me and, for no particular reason, haul off and punch me in the arm. As I got older and bigger, I would punch him back. Naturally, that's the part my parents would see, so I would be chewed out and Al got the last laugh. It's the same in sports. The one who hits last, or retaliates, is the one who gets called for the foul or ends up in the penalty box.

Al invented a game. He would say, "Let's see who can punch the softest. You go first." So, I would make like I was going to hit him hard, then at the last second, I would hold back and tap him lightly on the arm. Then, with a big smile, I'd say, "Your turn." Al would then wind up like Giants' pitcher Juan Marichal, complete with the high-kicking motion, pull his arm all the way back, and punch me as hard as he possibly could. As I was on the verge of tears, he'd say, "You win."

By about the tenth time we played this game, I caught on.

Marv, as the eldest of the three brothers, often served as the referee, breaking up the punch fests between Al and me. A truce was declared whenever we practiced our announcing.

Growing up with two brothers can result in an identity crisis. I was often mistaken for them. To make matters worse, I had an aunt who called me Ambrose, my pet hamster's name. I'm still trying to figure that one out.

Whenever my mother tried to get my attention, she would call out my brothers' names first. For example, she would shout out in rapid-fire fashion, "Marv, Al, Steve—take out the garbage!" or "Marv, Al, Steve—make your bed!" To be clear, she was not telling all three of us to take out the garbage or make our beds, just me. For some unknown reason, she needed to tightly conjoin our names, my brothers' before mine. I got used to it.

I'm sometimes asked, how is it that an incredibly shy, self-effacing kid like me would go into such an ego-driven business? I didn't fit the image.

In many families, younger siblings follow in the footsteps of their brothers or sisters, and sons and daughters have been known to do what their fathers or mothers do.

As a child, you may see what brings joy and happiness to other family members, or perhaps you see an occupation in a practical sense, as a way to make a living and provide for your family.

A Funny Thing Happened on the Way to the Broadcast Booth

In my case, I observed my brothers' passion for sports at an early age and simply fell head over heels for it, just as they had. I believe deep down that we probably wanted to grow up to play sports professionally, but each of us had a reality check. We could take our athletic skills only so far. Al went the farthest as a minor league hockey player. In my case, it was the schoolyard. Same for Marv. So, we decided to do the next best thing and announce the games.

In entering the "family business," so to speak, you are automatically subject to comparisons. Some occupations are more public than others, which adds a whole different dimension to the comparisons. Instead of whispers about you at the office water cooler, they're being shouted in newspapers and magazines, or, today, on social media.

Broadcasting is pretty public.

At the time we were training at home for our futures, I was too young and naïve to understand the concept of being compared to someone else. Why would people do that, and what was the satisfaction they gained from it? The notion of judging someone else hadn't entered my thinking yet, nor the thought of escaping someone's shadow.

When I arrived in New York as a young sportscaster, Marv was becoming the toast of the town. He had already established his prominence as Marty Glickman's heir apparent with his dynamic play-by-play calls of the Knicks' 1970 NBA championship. He was steadily becoming the most visible sports voice in the Big Apple.

Al had left New York to become the TV play-by-play announcer for the Denver Nuggets. Therefore, I was now the only brother working in Marv's shadow. Being compared to Marv meant I was being compared to the best. I was still wet behind the ears, but I understood at this point that people were going to be judgmental, and their views were magnified under the New York microscope. If that wasn't enough, claims of nepotism also surfaced. I wasn't the first person to deal with all this junk, and I wouldn't be the last.

It's All Relative

Being the youngest of three sportscasting brothers had its pluses and minuses. Sure, an older brother can open some doors, but you have to keep your foot in it yourself. And, escaping your brothers' shadows can be a challenge. It's all how you deal with it.

As I learned, life is hard sometimes, and you either contend with it or you let it take you down. I decided to contend with it the best way I could. That way was to work harder.

You can't control what other people say or think, but if you do your job to the best of your ability, you can forge your own success.

If a stranger says to you, "You're no so-and-so" or "You'll never be as good as so-and-so," guess what? That's his or her problem, not yours. If it makes a person feel better by saying those things, so be it. It's no reflection on you. If that ever happens, just smile and walk away. If that doesn't work, try a left hook to the jaw.

In all candor, if I didn't want to be judged or compared to someone else, then I would not have gone into broadcasting. Everybody's got an opinion, so you need to develop a thick skin.

The next time somebody asks me, "Are you any relation to your brother Marv?" I'll say, "I'm not only related to my brother Marv, I'm also related to my brother Al. And proud of it."

A Funny Thing Happened on the Way to the Broadcast Booth

Epilogue: After the Broadcast Booth

One of the best purchases I made after retiring was a booth. Not a broadcast booth, but a standard-issue dining booth from a restaurant supply store.

There's nothing like a good old-fashioned diner. The one where the waitstaff know your name, the pancake stacks are tall and the bacon crisp, and the menu is a mile long, filled with reliable classics like the "Hungry Man Special."

I wanted to bring that comforting diner experience home.

I think that's part of why I loved sports. Every game had a familiar and comfortable feel to it. What I miss most about announcing for a team are the friendships and camaraderie I built with the other announcers, the production crew, the ushers, and the fans. I also miss the exhilaration of calling the play-by-play—a pinpoint pass, a chase-down block, or a three-point shot to win a game at the buzzer—and the feeling of satisfaction I got from nailing the description of a play.

When you're in the midst of your career, retirement is something you don't think about. Then, out of nowhere, it sneaks up on you. The cheering stops, and suddenly it's time to move on.

Writing this book allowed me to not only recapture my youth but to relive my adventures as a sportscaster.

I hope you enjoyed reading my stories as much as I enjoyed writing them. Now, it's time to enjoy some fun times and good food from my dining booth.

My fellow booth companions—Chompie and Nena

Acknowledgments

The idea for my book actually started about twenty years ago while I was sitting on an airplane doing, what else, preparing for my next play-by-play broadcast. I would jot down notes for the book on a legal pad, then get back to my game preparation. Eventually, the games won out, and the book idea wound up collecting dust on a shelf. My busy schedule kept getting in the way.

It took retirement and a global pandemic to reignite the fire.

To my brothers, Marv Albert and Al Albert, thank you for the early training, and for opening a door that would prepare me for a life in the broadcast booth.

To my parents, who supported our ambitions to be sportscasters, going as far as changing our last name to help the cause. Beyond all the "parenty" things they did for me, I'm also thankful to my father, Max Albert, for showing me the importance of humility, and to my mother, Alida Albert, for inspiring my offbeat sense of humor with hers. And thanks to my once and always home of Brooklyn, not just a borough, but a state of mind.

Gratitude goes out to my entire family and all my friends for their encouragement throughout this undertaking. They all contributed to this book, in one form or another. Many thanks as well to my business managers, Evan Bell and Liza de Leon, who have been by my side for decades.

I am thankful to all the organizations with whom I worked, from Showtime to the New York/New Jersey Nets to all the TV news stations. I particularly want to acknowledge the Cleveland Crusaders for giving me my first full-time job and the Phoenix Suns for giving me a chance in the eleventh hour of my career.

Much appreciation to Pete Grossman for introducing me to developmental editor Rich Mintzer, who helped me convert this work from memoir style into a book of predominantly sports humor. On top of that, Rich connected me with copy and line editor Sara Putnam, whose honesty, wisdom, research abilities, and attention to detail were a gift. Sara then turned me over to Linda LiDestri, proofreader extraordinaire.

Last but not least, love and gratefulness to my partner Nena Wong for selflessly sacrificing many hours of her time to help me complete this project. She also assisted with the editing of the book. As cliche as it sounds, I could not have done it without her. And Nena wouldn't forgive me if I didn't mention our endlessly entertaining sheepadoodle Chompie, who never once rejected my stories when I first tried them out on her and barked for joy when I finally finished writing. That meant more time for belly rubs and long walks outside.

About the Author

Steve Albert comes from a family of sportscasters. His older brothers Marv and Al are well known for their decades of work in the business and his nephew Kenny carries on the tradition.

Steve started his career announcing for the Cleveland Crusaders of the World Hockey Association and transitioned to basketball, calling New York Nets games in the American Basketball Association. He called the historic final ABA championship, featuring the legendary Julius Erving, aka Dr. J. The Nets role evolved into a 24-year run in the NBA with the New Jersey Nets, Golden State Warriors, New Orleans Hornets and Phoenix Suns. He was named the top sports announcer in Arizona by the *Arizona Republic* and won an Emmy Award for his play-by-play.

Alongside his NBA work, Steve announced professional boxing nationally for over 25 years, 23 of them for *Showtime Championship Boxing*, calling countless marquee fights. He did blow-by-blow for over 300 world title bouts, including the infamous Mike Tyson-Evander Holyfield Bite Fight to an audience of millions.

That led to Steve's induction into the prestigious International Boxing Hall of Fame. Steve was also inducted into the World Boxing Hall of Fame and the New York State Boxing Hall of Fame. He received the coveted Sam Taub Award for Excellence in Boxing Broadcast Journalism from the Boxing Writers Association of America and was twice named Announcer of the Year by the International Boxing Federation.

Amidst all of his play-by-play duties, Steve was a sports anchor at WCBS-TV, WNBC- TV, WOR-TV (now WWOR-TV) and WABC radio in New York.

Earlier in his career, he announced for the New York Mets, the New York Islanders, and the New York Jets. Steve has also appeared in numerous movies, television dramas and sitcoms, along with many TV and radio commercials.

He was the host and play-by-play announcer for the long-running MTV *Rock n' Jock* series, working with dozens of major celebrities and sports stars. Steve's diverse career included the nationally televised call of daredevil Robbie Knievel's motorcycle jump over the fountains of Caesars Palace and play-by-play in the iconic Sesame Street video, *Elmo's Potty Time*. He also hosted two nationally syndicated sports competition game shows, *The Grudge Match* and *Battle Dome*.

Steve graduated from Kent State University with a bachelor of science degree in telecommunications. While in college, he started the Kent State hockey team.

Steve retired from a 45-year career as a sportscaster in 2017.

About the Author

www.ingramcontent.com/pod-product-compliance
Lightning Source LLC
LaVergne TN
LVHW051824080426
835512LV00018B/2711